Men and Battle
Anzio:
Edge of Disaster

ANZIO:

A Talisman / Parrish Book

EDGE OF DISASTER

William Lusk Allen

Elsevier-Dutton
New York

To
Don W. Lusk
and
Myron H. Allen

Grateful acknowledgment is made to the publishers of the following books
for the use of quoted material.

Winston S. Churchill, *Closing the Ring* (Houghton Mifflin Company)
Mark W. Clark, *Calculated Risk* (Harper & Row)
Bill Mauldin, *Up Front* (Holt, Rinehart & Winston)
Ernie Pyle, *Brave Men* (Holt, Rinehart & Winston)

Copyright © 1978 by Talisman/Parrish Books, Inc.

ISBN: 0-525-93003-5

*Published in the United States by E. P. Dutton,
a Division of Sequoia-Elsevier Publishing Company, Inc., New York
Published simultaneously in Canada by
Clarke, Irwin & Company Limited, Toronto and Vancouver*

*Art Direction: The Etheredges
Production Manager: Stephen Konopka*

Printed in the U.S.A.   First Edition
10 9 8 7 6 5 4 3 21

Contents

Preface

The drama of Anzio is really two stories—the story of GIs and the story of generals. The Allied commanders at the top had an unusual series of doubts, disagreements and clashes of will and idea. The infantrymen had to survive the mind- and body-punishing pressures resulting from their being pinned in place and then almost being pushed into the sea. The long struggle for this tiny bit of the coast of Italy was well out of proportion to its size, and the necessity of the operation will always be argued by military historians. Perhaps this book will at least provide a context for those interested in the question. In fact, the story of Anzio is not complete if one does not know how it fits into the overall military situation of that time. Not only must the reader have some familiarity with the background of the Allied landing in Italy, he must be very much aware of activity related directly to Anzio—concerted but unsuccessful Allied attempts to fracture the Germans' Gustav Line which had been drawn defensively across southern Italy. The line's sole purpose was to keep the Allies at bay, away from the Italian capital, and for several months it did just that. Anzio was in reality a secondary effort to lessen German presence at the Gustav Line so that it might be more easily breached by our forces. Thus contextually the two fighting arenas go hand-in-hand. Although this volume is mostly about

Anzio, it covers in some detail the entire Allied advance, stalemate and advance again before the entry into Rome. It may be useful to state here that in describing these operations, times of day are given according to the military system, in which the hours are numbered consecutively from midnight as the start of the day (thus 0200 is 2 A.M.).

Acknowledgments

One of the pleasant aspects of writing this book has been the willing support provided by several agencies and people who were called upon to help locate suitable reference material—in particular, the U.S. Army Center of Military History, the U.S. Army Military History Institute, and the Silver City, New Mexico, Public Library, all tied together by a slender but vital thread for the researcher, the Interlibrary Loan System. Whoever thought up the latter has my enduring thanks. At the Silver City Public Library, Mrs. Helen Lundwall, librarian; Mrs. Dorothy Hill, assistant librarian; Mrs. Katherine White, clerk; Miss Sharon Davis, library technician; and Miss Betty Ramirez, head page, all provided assistance above and beyond the call of duty. My uncomplaining typist, Norma Harrison, deserves special praise for the high quality of her work and for never being late with a much-needed chapter. Of all those who helped, I am most grateful to my wife, Arlene, researcher, writer and editor. Her help made the job of writing this book a distinct pleasure.

WILLIAM L. ALLEN

1. The Battle of the Caves

The battle was raging into its second day, and there was no sign of a letup. A German soldier was hanging wounded on the concertina wire entanglement that helped protect the 2d Battalion's perimeter, and every once in a while he cried out in English, "My name is Müller, I am wounded." Neither German nor American made a move to help the gray-green-uniformed grenadier, even though his plea continued unabated throughout the day. Both sides were busy. The Germans were launching assault after fanatical assault, and the Americans were fending them off with equal determination. As day turned to night, during the rare lulls in the din of battle, Müller's plaintive call could be heard by some of the battalion defenders: "My name is Müller, I am wounded." For more than 24 hours this pain-racked chant kept the listeners on edge, but finally it became unbearable. A hand grenade was unloosed from its keeper, its pin was pulled by a tired hand and as it was thrown there was an "almost silent mutter: 'What's your name now, you son of a . . .'" The question trailed off and was accentuated by the explosion of the grenade. For a brief moment there was silence. Then the battle resumed around the isolated American battalion.

This unit belonged to the 45th Infantry Division—a National Guard

1

Cave system resembles a two-room apartment

outfit whose men hailed from New Mexico, Oklahoma, Colorado and Arizona—commanded at this point by Major General W. W. Eagles. Along with the others of the 157th Infantry Regiment, the 2d Battalion was fighting for its life near the final beachhead line surrounding the port of Anzio, Italy. The Germans were trying to drive the Americans—and their British allies—back into the Tyrrhenian Sea from which they had landed a little less than a month earlier. It was now 16 February 1944.

The 2d Battalion held a sector in the defense that would soon become part of the left shoulder of an extremely serious German penetration of the Allied lines. Its sister battalions were occupying equally critical positions. Just before the enemy onslaught began, the 2d Battalion, with Lieutenant Colonel Laurence C. Brown in command, was assigned a front of about 2,000 yards, beginning some 500 yards west of the Albano road and extending into the rough, broken country that formed the headwaters of the Moletta River. Company E was on the right, Company F in the center and Company G on the left; H Company was in reserve.

This particular piece of land was important to the Allies because its possession denied the Germans the use of a network of dirt roads leading into the Allied final defense line. The area to the rear of the battalion's foxholes and slit trenches, known locally as the Caves of Pozzolana, was a system of shepherd's caverns that had been dug into a ridge line. Some were connected by tunnels, and the largest of them served as Colonel

2

Brown's command post. Since there were thousands of yards of caves, most of which were impervious to enemy artillery fire and some of them as large as garages, there was plenty of room for supply points, infirmaries and places to keep prisoners. To the front of the battalion's position stretched miles of flat land broken only by ditches hardly deep enough to conceal a man crawling.

There was no question that the enemy was coming on in earnest at dawn on the 16th. First came the artillery—the whine as the shells approached and the crash when they struck. GIs in their dugouts and trenches grew tense as the barrage increased in tempo, and between noises could be heard cries for the medics. To Brown's men it seemed as if the shelling continued forever, but as suddenly as it had come on, it stopped. The rumble of armor became the predominant sound as German tanks followed by infantry bore down on the battalion, centering on the soldiers of Company E. The Americans were able to stop many of the German grenadiers with rifles and machine guns, but three of the enemy tanks could not at first be halted, and they almost immediately overran one of Company E's platoons. One of the two supporting American tank destroyers had been knocked out during the first enemy rush, but its mate lived up to its name by knocking out two of the tanks that were decimating the American foot-bound soldiers. Suddenly the remaining tank withdrew, leaving the German infantry to carry on the battle. The lone tank destroyer then trained its .50-caliber machine guns on the enemy soldiers, at almost point-blank range, and sent them scurrying for cover. Many Germans were killed before the destroyer had to retire to replenish its ammunition, leaving the E Company infantrymen to fend for themselves. Such was the scene all morning as wave after wave of Germans repeated the performance. They died by the hundreds, but they never stopped coming.

The attack hit Company G with almost equal force. Tanks were immobilized by Allied artillery, but the German infantry continued to advance, crawling through the shallow ditches where necessary. On the right flank of the company about 200 enemy soldiers died before reaching the perimeter, but on the left a platoon was overrun. So bad was the onslaught that the company commander, First Lieutenant Joe Robertson, called artillery fire in on his own positions, causing some American casualties but slaughtering the enemy. This was followed by hand-to-hand combat as the Germans poured into foxholes and trenches, finally forcing the remainder of the hard-hit platoon to withdraw.

There was no doubt by midday that this was it: the do or die effort of the Germans to drive the Allies from Anzio. According to one history, "The fury of the German assault was almost unbelievable . . . 16 different regiments were identified . . . Seven divisions were used . . . [to fight] in the Campo di Carne—which, ironically enough, translated means 'Field of Meat.' "

Noon came and went with no respite for the 2d Battalion. Another platoon was overrun; its antitank guns had been destroyed, enabling the tanks to fire almost directly into the infantrymen's positions at point-blank range. Some men were dazed from the constant explosions, all were defenseless against the tanks, and many were forced to give themselves up. Dusk of the first day brought a slowing of the attack, but it did not altogether stop. Throughout the night infiltrators moved into various battalion positions, clawing at the handful of men who were holding on.

By daylight of the second day—before Müller began his eerie chant—Company E found itself with only 18 men remaining, and began a withdrawal from forward positions. Also at dawn, the Germans resumed their relentless offensive. Company G seemed to be the focal point this day, but enemy infantrymen were stopped by an accurate crossfire that left scattered groups of dead and wounded in front of the American positions. According to a 45th Division history, "At one point, an odd-shaped X formed by dead Germans showed where machine gunners had laid down their fire." All day the Germans took advantage of every break, and their artillery, too, was effective as it rained ceaselessly on the battalion's wavering perimeter. Enemy infantrymen were also there, and in the confusion of battle fired at any target of opportunity.

Medics of the 2d Battalion were kept constantly on the move and, setting up an aid station in the caves to the rear, treated the wounded as best they could. Supplies of all kinds were short—even water. The 45th Division history says,

U.S. 155-mm "Long Tom" takes part in the February fighting

"Water was needed, but only occasionally could carriers work their way forward to the caves. In a nearby draw trickled a stream in which lay corpses of enemy dead. The water ran blood red, but many of the men filled their canteens, boiled the water and drank."

G Company was forced to withdraw to the caves that day, and as Müller began his nighttime pleading Colonel Brown received a warning that German infiltrators were getting too close to the command post. The caves became one of the defensive positions as the enemy troops, alone or in pairs, moved around seemingly at will. Although using their side arms effectively, the Americans found it necessary once again to call artillery in on their positions. As the Germans got close enough to lob hand grenades into the command post, the Allied batteries trained their howitzers in the direction of the caves, firing steadily for two hours. According to one source who was there,

"fighting from inside the caves was a nightmare. Each rifle shot echoed and re-echoed off the walls and ceilings and floors of the chambers and connecting passages and sounded more like the report of a cannon than of a .30-caliber M-1, and German machine-pistol fire and exploding potato mashers kept the defenders well back from the mouths of the caves, adding to the cacophonous racket inside. In lulls between enemy attacks, the men busied themselves refilling M-1 clips by stripping now useless machine gun belts, and they listened to the chatter of the German prisoners huddled in the corner of one of the larger caves, where they were out of the line of fire."

Although the 2d Battalion was isolated most of the time, at first relief occasionally got through. The night of the 18th, after an attack forward by the 6th Armored Infantry Regiment, 1st Armored Division, men of the 2d Battalion found a possible route for resupply to replace the one cut off by the Germans. That night drivers and carriers from the rear brought ammunition to the caves and forward positions and, while under fire, were able to evacuate about 100 casualties. Then the Germans closed in once more, and the battalion was now cut off. The two companies that had brought in the supplies had to fight their way back to the final beachhead line.

Fighting in the 2d Battalion sector for the next three days was somewhat less desperate than previously. Although at times very bitter, the struggle was characterized by intermittent shelling accompanied by light, local attacks against the Americans that were generally repulsed with comparative ease. Then, late in the afternoon of the 21st, the Germans began once more to infiltrate—very effectively—the battalion defenses. Soon the fighting became close, first with small arm against small arm, then hand-to-hand, all the way into the command post.

At this point, a plan of the British 56th Division—also on line at Anzio—to relieve the shattered and entirely surrounded 2d Battalion was

5

put into effect. Because of the intense fighting already under way, however, execution of this plan was doomed to partial failure. Men of the 2/7 Queens Battalion did reach the caves that night, but on the way they met considerable opposition in the form of enemy bombers, artillery and infantry. Tanks and antitank guns sent to help the British were destroyed, and by the time the Queens reached the Americans they had suffered 70 casualties and were without supplies, ammunition or supporting weapons. Nevertheless, the men in the caves "welcomed them with heartfelt joy," as the history says. When the British began to take over some of the American positions that guarded the avenues of approach to the caves, they had to be furnished with American weapons. Just as they were settling in, the Germans attacked again. Once more an artillery concentration was called for on the Allied positions, and the enemy assault was finally stopped. But it became impossible for the men of the 2d Battalion to try to pull out.

On the 22d the fighting continued almost without letup as the British finished their occupation of the American positions. Colonel Brown's exhausted men were well aware that they would have to fight their way back to Allied lines, but they were eager to try. Not until 0130 the next day did Brown feel that he could make a run for it. Then, in extreme darkness, with his battalion formed in a column of companies, the colonel and his men slipped out of the caves and headed south. The file had made it nearly halfway when the enemy from well-entrenched positions unloaded on the hapless Americans. Men ran for cover as deadly machine gun fire raked the column, splitting it into many smaller bodies of infantrymen who would now have to get back as best they could. The first half of the battalion, which included Colonel Brown, made it to safety with relative ease. During the rest of the night, and all the next day under the cover of smoke, other men filtered back to the lines. One company commander was left with no one in his unit except a sergeant, who made it back after two days spent with the British. That man was Sergeant Leon Siehr, who said, simply,

> "We were bringing up the rear of the column. Something happened. We were all pretty tired. Anyway, we lost contact. We got the order to stay where we were while officers moved forward and tried to reach the lead troops. We were catching a lot of fire from machine guns. Nobody came back, so Sergeant Garcia took off to try to find a way out. He disappeared, too, like the others."

Colonel Brown's infantrymen had held against overwhelming odds for a week. Only 225 men of the battalion made it back, and of these, 90 had to be hospitalized. Some had lost their hearing, mostly because of the loud mortar and artillery fire they had had to undergo almost constantly, and others could hardly walk. According to the official history, "That any man returned is a tribute to the courage and stamina of the American infantry

Captured Germans file by American foxholes

soldiers who have made the battle of the caves an epic of defensive fighting."

In an unhappy epilogue to the 2d Battalion's tenacity, the Queens Battalion, suffering just as fearfully and also completely surrounded, was able to hold out for only two days. Then an enemy tank and infantry attack of surprising determination closed the circle on what was left of a British unit that had suffered severe losses, even before taking over at the caves. Only a few of the British got back to their lines. The enemy completed his occupation of the bulge in the western shoulder of the salient. The official history sums it up this way:

"The battle of the caves did not end the fighting on the left shoulder. It was merely the most important and most costly action in a bloody war of attrition in which whole squads and platoons disappeared without leaving a trace."

7

2. North Africa to the Rapido

It was a long way from Anzio, in both time and distance, when late in 1942 northwest Africa was invaded by the Anglo-American allies. Called Torch, this operation was part of a concerted ground offensive in the Mediterranean. On the other side of Africa, at El Alamein, the British Eighth Army had, a little more than two weeks previously, begun an offensive against the German-Italian Army and was beginning to move westward. This effort, a turning point in Britain's wartime fortunes, was being carried out under the general charge of the British Commander in Chief, Middle East, General Sir Harold Alexander. The Torch attack, under Lieutenant General Dwight D. Eisenhower, opened with landings at Casablanca, Oran and Algiers. The Axis forces in North Africa were thus caught squarely between two Allied armies. On 10 May 1943, compressed into the Cap Bon peninsula in Tunisia, they surrendered to the Allies.

A question that had already been settled by the time of this victory was that Sicily would be the next objective of the Allied offensive in the Mediterranean. At the Casablanca conference in January 1943, the Americans and the British had agreed that they were not ready to invade Europe across the English Channel. Sicily, with its airfields, was a logical choice. Its capture would help the Allies secure uncontested control of the Mediterranean. President Franklin D. Roosevelt and Prime Minister Winston Churchill had made no decision about operations after Sicily, but various alternatives were discussed. Anzio was still a long way off. The Sicilian operation was code-named Husky.

Even before Sicily was invaded, however, events were taking place that would force the Allies to continue their drive in the Mediterranean. Actually, President Roosevelt and the American staff were proponents of a cross-Channel invasion of France as soon as possible. But Churchill and the British, on the other hand, believed that more effort should be made in the Mediterranean—the cherished theory of invading the Continent through its "soft underbelly." In May 1943 a compromise agreement was worked out. A cross-Channel attack (Overlord) was to be launched on 1 May 1944, and steps were to be taken to eliminate Italy from the war immediately.

General Eisenhower was enjoined in his campaign against Italy to use only those forces already in the Mediterranean, less seven divisions that had to be transferred to the United Kingdom on 1 November 1943. He was directed to "plan such operations in exploitation of Husky as are best calculated to eliminate Italy from the war and to contain the maximum number of German forces." The Combined Chiefs of Staff (CCS) reserved for the future the choice of which of several alternatives beyond Sicily would be adopted.

Roosevelt (l.) and Churchill disagreed on Mediterranean emphasis

Churchill was keenly disappointed that the Allies were not explicitly committed to an invasion of Italy, and he was convinced that if such a tack were taken it might make the cross-Channel attack and the direct invasion of Germany unnecessary. In an effort to influence the planning beyond Sicily, he met with the Americans in Algiers late in May. There he pushed for an invasion of the Italian mainland. Since the outcome of Husky was an unknown—the operation was actually still a few weeks away—Eisenhower said that only if the island fell quickly could immediate operations be undertaken against the mainland.

Other events at this time influenced the issue of where to invade. On 25 July Mussolini was forced by the King of Italy to resign as head of the government. In his place the King appointed Marshal Pietro Badoglio, who was deeply loyal to the King and who, like the King, wanted to get out of the war. Through diplomatic channels contact was made with representatives of General Eisenhower, who later wrote, "The Italians wanted frantically to surrender. However, they wanted to do so only with the assurance that such a powerful Allied force would land on the mainland simultaneously with their surrender that the government itself and their cities would enjoy complete protection from the German forces."

Thus, with the fall of Mussolini, the imminent Italian surrender, and the ease with which Sicily was being captured, a decision by the Allies to undertake a major campaign on the mainland became more of a certainty. There were yet other positive considerations. An Allied occupation of southern Italy would provide air bases close to Germany and the Balkans and would force Hitler to tie down many German troops, preventing their use against the Russians on the eastern front or against the Allies when they attacked across the Channel a year hence. Since the U.S. and British governments had decided to eliminate Italy by whatever way proved best, an invasion of the mainland was becoming more logical every day, and American planners resigned themselves to that fact. Then the Italian government agreed to a surrender, which was announced officially by Eisenhower on 8 September. Italy, though, had already been invaded at one location, and two other landings were to follow. General Sir Bernard Montgomery had slipped two divisions of the Eighth Army across the Strait of Messina on the night of 3 September. As Eisenhower wrote later, "the invasion of the Continent of Europe was an accomplished fact."

It was four years to the day after Britain had gone to war. In an operation called Baytown, Montgomery's Canadian 1st and British 5th Divisions, with armor, infantry and Commando reinforcements, moved quickly across the strait into Calabria. Allied aircraft hit gun positions all over the toe of Italy and struck strategically located airfields, railway yards and road junctions while the Commonwealth units made the first landings. Together with the air support came a massive artillery bombardment, as 600 Army and Navy guns—some 14 warships were on hand just offshore—delivered their fire. The preparation may have been unnecessary. There was practically no resistance from either the Germans or the Italians. It soon became evident that it would not be the enemy troops that slowed down the British advance northward, but that the terrain and German demolition work would do the job.

As for the Americans, various alternatives in Italy had been in the planning stages for many weeks. One involved the seizure of Naples, another concerned a landing on the heel of Italy. On 26 July, Lieutenant General Mark W. Clark, commander of the newly formed U.S. Fifth Army and former deputy to General Eisenhower, received a "planning task" known as Avalanche. This one called for an amphibious assault in the vicinity of Naples, most likely in the Bay of Salerno. General Clark, who liked the idea, directed his staff to get to work on it right away. Although the date of Avalanche depended on the outcome in Sicily and the possibility of an Italian surrender, Clark was sure there would be a battle, for the Germans would fight regardless of what happened with the Italians in the political arena.

Making up the Fifth Army during this period were the American VI Corps, which included the 34th and 36th Infantry Divisions, the 1st Armored Division and the 82d Airborne Division; and the British X Corps, consisting of the 46th and 56th Infantry Divisions and the 1st Airborne Division. The Fifth Army, its two corps, and most of the divisions had their work cut out for them, for not only would they see severe action at Salerno, but they would also take part in the operations at Cassino and Anzio, and only then after a very long and difficult road.

One of the fortunes of war, blossoming to full use in mid-1943, was that the Allies—operating out of a center in England—had succeeded in defeating Germany's most sophisticated code system. Just before the war broke out the Polish Secret Service had obtained an exact copy of the highly secret and complex coding machine known as Enigma. Months later, the supposedly unbreakable Enigma system was beaten with the help of another very complicated machine. Thereafter, and with increasing frequency owing to refinements in procedures, high-level coded signals were made available to the Allied commanders. This intelligence was code-named Ultra. Information derived from Ultra had been used to good advantage in North Africa and was to be of great value in Italy and during the invasion of France. The contents of most of the secret wireless messages between Hitler and his commanders were usually in the hands of the Allies before the Germans could carry out their plans, and, in some cases, Allied leaders were actually aware of Hitler's orders before the German generals in the field had even received them.

Because of Ultra and other intelligence information, the Allies had knowledge of the enemy's situation on the Italian mainland. One message received and decoded in August reported the position of the German divi-

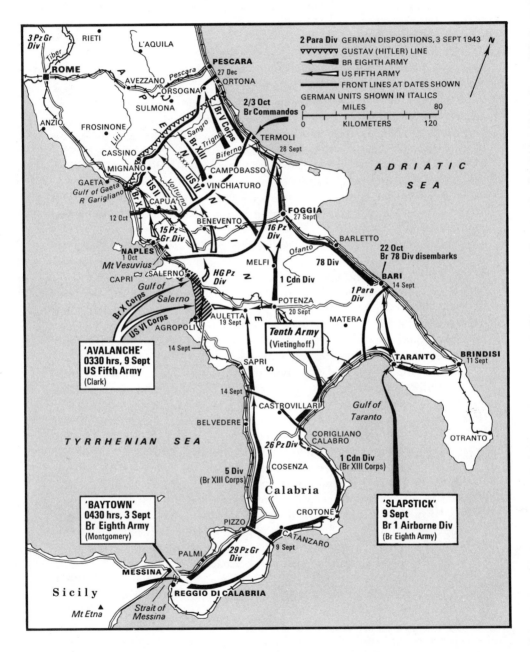

THE ALLIES LAND IN ITALY

sions in southern Italy, those under the command of the senior German commander in Italy, Generalfeldmarschall (Field Marshal) Albert Kesselring, Commander in Chief South (OB SÜD). Generaloberst (Colonel General) Heinrich von Vietinghoff, the commander of the newly formed Tenth Army, as well as his chief, Kesselring, had a considerable number of forces available in central and southern Italy to meet an Allied invasion. Under the Tenth Army were the LXXVI Panzer Corps with its two units, the 26th Panzer and 29th Panzer Grenadier Divisions (30,000 men), which were withdrawing from Calabria; the XIV Panzer Corps, some 45,000 men strong, consisting of the Hermann Göring Division, the 15th Panzer Grenadier Division and the 16th Panzer Division, which were deployed along the coast between Gaeta and Salerno; and the 17,000-man 1st Parachute Division, which would more than prove its mettle at Cassino but which was now stationed around Foggia. In the Rome area, under XI Flieger Corps, were the 3d Panzer Grenadier Division and the 2d Parachute Division. Fortunately for the Allies, the Germans had not broken the Allied code; prior to Montgomery's landing Kesselring was not at all sure where the Allied invasion would take place. He could rule out the Balkans, but for Italy he surmised only that the site was "entirely unpredictable." Vietinghoff, on the other hand, even before he assumed command of the Tenth Army, had concluded that "Allied landings in the Naples-Salerno sector represent the main danger to the whole of the German forces in Italy."

Planning for Avalanche, the amphibious operation at Salerno, continued rapidly during August. General Clark selected the 36th Division, commanded by an old friend, Major General Fred Walker, for the main thrust at Salerno because it had "good leadership and high caliber personnel." Clark, however, did not feel quite so confident about the VI Corps commander, Major General Ernest J. Dawley, who had reluctantly been accepted by Eisenhower when nominated for the command by the War Department. By mid-August, General Alexander had approved the Fifth Army plan for Avalanche, which included an airdrop of 82d Airborne Division troops northwest of Naples along the Volturno River. This plan was approved by Eisenhower on 23 August at a conference at Algiers, where all present—including Alexander and Montgomery—agreed that the Eighth Army invasion at Calabria would be diversionary and the Fifth Army's amphibious assault over the beaches at Salerno would be the Allied main effort in Italy.

On 3 September, the same day as the Eighth Army crossed over to the mainland, a hitch developed in Clark's plans, when Ike revealed that the 82d Airborne Division could not be used in Avalanche. The Italian surrender political situation required that the division be dropped on Rome to assist the Italians in holding the capital until Allied forces could land and relieve it. The conversation went like this:

13

EISENHOWER: "It will be a shock to you, but it has been decided that we'll make the drop on Rome."

CLARK, who didn't yet understand why it should be a shock: "Where are you going to get an airborne division to do it?"

EISENHOWER: "The Eighty-second."

CLARK: "No. That's my division."

Clark's subsequent argument—essentially a recounting of the need for the division on the Volturno—met with failure. This turn of events may well have been a blessing, as will be seen. For the present, though discouraged by this unplanned development, Clark felt some consolation in the fact that if the Italians refused to fight, Avalanche might be less difficult than expected.

Convoys sailed from Fifth Army headquarters, from Bizerte, from Tripoli and from Palermo on the 6th, all bound for the rendezvous off the Bay of Salerno. Clark was relieved to be on his way at last. He now had his first battle command. He surmised that there could well be one of two extremes in Fifth Army's fortunes. "At best, we could steam into Naples Harbor [sic] unopposed. At worst, we could have a hell of a fight."

About that same time Alexander cabled Churchill concerning General Montgomery's progress in the south. The Prime Minister, who was occupied with Overlord strategy at the Allied Quadrant conference in Quebec, was told that in the Eighth Army area there was little indication that a war was even going on. The ships plying back and forth between Sicily and the mainland, Alexander said, were "more like a regatta in peacetime."

During this time, while everything else was going on, General Eisenhower had been planning another and relatively impromptu operation called Slapstick. A quick movement of British paratroopers by boat to Taranto, inside the heel of Italy, Slapstick was intended simply to capitalize on the many events taking place that, it was hoped, were confusing the enemy. Theoretically, an additional operation would make it more difficult for the Germans to come up with a sound defensive plan. So quick was the Slapstick planning that General Alexander remarked that even the code name illustrated its extempore nature. In any case, shipping resources were available, and 3,600 troops of the British 1st Airborne Division sailed into Taranto harbor on 9 September, the same day as the Salerno landings. There were no Germans in the city, and the Italians, who were manning the port defenses, welcomed the new arrivals. Since the port was intact, the British soon organized the facilities. Two days later members of the 1st Airborne Division occupied without opposition the port of Brindisi, on the Adriatic side of Italy.

To the men engaged in battle at Salerno, however, the progress of Montgomery's Eighth Army was much more of a concern. The army continued to move north slowly, partly, at least, because of the skillful German

14

Lieutenant General
Mark W. Clark

delaying tactics and the rugged terrain. If the Germans escaped this British advance, which seemed quite likely, and were able to reinforce in the Salerno area, then the Fifth Army might well realize that "hell of a fight" that General Clark wondered about.

Eisenhower's announcement of the Italian surrender on 8 September, the eve of the Salerno operation, was made amid political confusion. Since the Italians could not guarantee that they could assist the 82d Airborne Division after it landed in Rome, as had been promised during the negotiations for surrender, the plans for using the division were suddenly scuttled. By then it was too late to use the paratroopers in Avalanche, and in any case General Clark would not receive word until 11 September that the division was back under his control. Although the vacillation of the Badoglio government during the final hours before the surrender did not cause a change in invasion plans, there was some cause for worry. Even though the Italian forces had been ordered by Marshal Badoglio to stop fighting the Allies and "oppose attacks from any other quarter," there was still some question as to how the Italian military—the battle fleet, for example— would react to the surrender. Would they fight or would they capitulate?

Avalanche became a reality when at 0330 on 9 September, elements of General Walker's 36th Division began their long, difficult trek up the Italian mainland by stepping on the shores at Salerno. To end any doubt in the minds of the Americans that the landing would come about unopposed by the Germans, a loudspeaker announced brashly in English: "Come on in and give up. You're covered."

15

The actual plans for this assault were rather simple, and according to General Eisenhower, the operation developed just about the way G-2 had said it would. The British X Corps—with three U.S. Ranger battalions under the command of Lieutenant Colonel William O. Darby, two British Commando units, and the 46th and 56th Divisions—was to land north of the Sele River, capture Salerno and its port, the Montecorvino airfield, Battipaglia and a Sele River bridge, some 14 miles upstream. The VI Corps was to land south of the Sele and secure the high ground, an arc of mountains that dominated the Salerno plain. There was also a floating reserve of two regiments of the 45th Division. After the reserve had landed, then the rest of the 45th, the 1st Armored and the 34th Divisions were to enter the mainland through the port of Naples, which was to be captured by that time. Also to land was the U.S. 3d Infantry Division, under the command of one of the officers who would become intimately involved at Anzio, Major General Lucian K. Truscott, Jr.

The 16th Panzer Division met the invasion force head-on, and immediately began to put up a good fight. A few of the Allied assault boats were unable to reach their designated landing areas and had to be shifted to others, men were separated from their weapons, and radio communication became difficult because of equipment losses and the intense fire. Nevertheless, the infantrymen held on and advanced, working their way slowly inland to a railway, which, south of the town of Salerno, paralleled the beaches. As the official history says: "To get to the railroad across the sand, the dunes, small swamps, irrigation ditches, rock walls, and patches of trees provided an individual adventure for each soldier, a hazardous journey under the fire of enemy machine guns, mortars, and artillery . . ." It was the individual infantryman who kept the tanks of the 16th Panzers, the only fully equipped enemy armored division in southern Italy, at bay during the critical morning hours of the 9th. One soldier killed a tank only after crawling under machine-gun bursts to a place where he could properly fire his rocket launcher. After piercing the tank's armor plate, he crept up to it and jammed a hand grenade into the same hole, killing the crew. Another trooper simply jumped on a tank and dropped a grenade into an open turret.

Slowly the beachhead began to get organized. The infantry, British and American, was moving inland while the beachmaster was getting the tangle of incoming traffic and supplies into some semblance of order. Even though General Clark thought the assault progressed very slowly, by nightfall of the first day he felt that the Fifth Army had accomplished about all it could. The first critical period was over. Darby's Rangers had taken the high ground above Maiori, the British were in Salerno and had patrols operating in Montecorvino and Battipaglia. The 36th Division, in its first battle, controlled the plain south of the Sele River, having penetrated inland, on the average, to about five miles. But there was a 10-mile gap between the two corps, which at the end of the day did not seem too serious to the Fifth Army commander. He knew, however, that it must be closed quickly.

The New York *Times* of 12 September announced the capture of Salerno. The Allies, it said, "are grinding their way inland in the face of unabated counter-attacks." If not exactly true in the beginning, the description soon became fact as the German reaction began to take the form of a determined attempt to drive the British and American invaders back into the Tyrrhenian Sea. German plans were quickly made. Units which had been opposing the Eighth Army's northerly advance were brought with as much speed as possible to the battle. Vietinghoff sent elements of the 29th Panzer Grenadiers, LXXVI Corps, into the fray on the southern half of the battlefield. Two divisions from the Naples and Gaeta areas, the 15th Panzer and the Hermann Göring Divisions (both of which had fought hard in Sicily and were being rehabilitated because of severe losses), along with the already battling 16th Panzers, were concentrated initially under the XIV Panzer Corps against the northern half of the battle area. Delayed because of fuel supply problems, the 29th Panzers were committed piecemeal, with the full division not on hand until the 12th. Consequently, after the first day the X Corps felt the brunt of the opposition, while activity in the VI Corps area was waning.

Amphibious invasion: one of war's most complex operations

Clark knew that there were two sensitive areas on the beachhead, the extreme left flank where the Rangers were operating, and the gap separating the two corps, a piece of low ground between the Sele River and Battipaglia. He directed the reinforcement of the Rangers, and moved the VI Corps's left boundary north of the river, thus giving the task of filling the gap to the U.S. corps. Units used to fill the void were two regiments of the 45th Division, brought ashore on 10 September. With these potential problem areas solved, the Fifth Army commander wired General Alexander that soon he would be able to attack north to Naples.

From the 10th to the 12th, German resistance began to stiffen as reinforcements arrived in increasing numbers. General Clark realized that his message to Alexander had been somewhat optimistic, because "from then on things began to happen." On the 11th, Clark once again reduced the X Corps zone of responsibility, and he again shifted VI Corps troops to the Sele River area to meet the increased threat. On this same day, Alexander wired Clark that the 82d Airborne Division was once again under Fifth Army control, to be used in any way deemed necessary.

Fighting on the 12th reached a high point all along the front as German reinforcements peaked to the maximum. Clark was worried because General Dawley had not taken steps to protect the critical VI Corps left flank from counterattacks, and when these attacks came he committed all the troops "in a cordon defense, leaving none in reserve." General Clark realized late on the 12th that the men "were getting into a very tight place." As the Germans pushed harder in the Sele sector, he considered the awful possibility that the Fifth Army might be driven back into the sea, which would be catastrophic indeed. Pondering the fact that he had not issued routine orders for the destruction of supplies and equipment in the event of an emergency—something every commander is supposed to do—Clark walked along the beach, feeling dirty, tired and worried. Finally he said to hell with it—no orders like that. "The only way they're going to get us off this beach is to push us, step by step, into the water."

Shortly after noon on the 13th, the Germans unleashed a series of attacks, with the greatest pressure being directed in the Sele River area, where General Vietinghoff had suddenly discovered the gap between the two corps. Elements of the 29th Panzer Grenadier and 16th Panzer Divisions came forth from Altavilla, Eboli and Battipaglia. The Germans believed, quite erroneously, that the Allies were evacuating. Clark and his men had been busy beforehand, however, taking steps to counter the panzer forces. One of Clark's moves was to send a letter by the hand of a fighter pilot courier to Major General Matthew B. Ridgway, 82d Airborne Division commander. The message went directly to the point. Clark said that the letter was an order, that he realized the time usually needed to prepare for a parachute drop, but that this was an exception. "I want you to make a drop within our lines (near Albanella) on the beachhead and I want you to make it tonight. This is a must." Ridgway answered, "Can do," and asked that ground and naval forces hold their fire during the time of the operation.

The afternoon and evening of the 13th were critical as the infantrymen of the 36th and 45th Divisions held on. The night was spent in reorganizing and tightening defenses. General Walker, for example, divided his area into three sectors, placed a brigadier general in charge of each and directed them to hold at all costs, to "fight it out on this position." Almost on schedule, men of the 82d were dropped on the beachhead, and by morning were fighting with the 36th Division. General Clark, while touring the front on the 14th, was seen doing his part, stopping to talk with troops at every opportunity, telling them: "We don't give another inch. This is it. Don't yield anything. We're here to stay." Assisted by an air attack that used every available Allied plane, and helped by vast amounts of artillery and naval gunfire, the infantry at last regained the initiative. On the night of the 14th more reinforcements arrived, and by the 15th the crisis was over—the Allies had held. General Walker would later describe the last few days as a "fearful time."

General Alexander visited Fifth Army headquarters on the 15th, expressing satisfaction with the outcome at Salerno. By message he informed the Prime Minister that he was happier with the situation than he had been even 24 hours earlier. On this same day Kesselring and Vietinghoff, realizing that they could not succeed, began to swing their entire defensive line to the north. By the 18th, Alexander was able to tell Churchill that the initiative had passed to the Allies. (Clark believed that the initiative had been regained on the 15th.) In a message to Eisenhower a few days later, Churchill repeated in his congratulations a quote from the Duke of Wellington after the Battle of Waterloo: "It was a damned close-run thing." In his own words, the Prime Minister continued, "but your policy of running risks has been vindicated . . . [S]end a message to Clark, who from all I hear has done wonders."

General Clark was concerned with other things—the move to Naples and beyond and the leadership situation in VI Corps. For some time he had been concerned about General Dawley's "capacity" and the consequent need for a change of command for the corps. Both Eisenhower and Alexander concurred with the Fifth Army commander, and Dawley was replaced by Major General John P. Lucas, whom we shall see in a key role at Anzio. Lucas, a West Point graduate, had been Eisenhower's personal deputy in North Africa and Sicily, and had served briefly as the II Corps commander in Sicily before taking over the VI Corps.

Meanwhile to the east, just a few days before the crisis at Salerno ended, soldiers of the British 1st Airborne Division, which had landed at Taranto, linked up with the Baytown forces—XIII Corps's Canadian 1st and British 5th Divisions, under General Montgomery. On the 16th, pa-

19

Field Marshal
Albert Kesselring

trols of the Eighth Army arrived at Salerno to make the first contact with their counterparts. A few days later, during Clark's advance to Naples, General Montgomery paid his first visit to the Fifth Army headquarters. There Clark and Montgomery met for the first time. Montgomery told of his extended supply lines, of his inability to help directly the Fifth Army in its advance to Naples and of the need for the Eighth Army to get moving to the Foggia airfields, an important Allied objective. As Montgomery was leaving, he paused and asked Clark whether he knew Alexander well. Clark answered no, and Montgomery replied, "Well, I do. From time to time you will get instructions from Alex that you won't understand. When you do, just tell him to go to hell." Clark said that he wouldn't be able to do that. Instead, when he found himself in that dilemma he would tell Montgomery, who could then tell Alexander for him. Montgomery, however, was transferred to England before the Anzio operation, leaving Clark with a first-hand opportunity to see just how ambiguous Alexander's orders could be. This is an important strand in the Anzio story.

The Allied drive to Naples was not an easy task, mostly because of the seemingly incessant rains and the superb delaying tactics of Kesselring and Vietinghoff. Small rear-guard units with machine guns were dug in on strategic hillsides, and Army columns were harassed by German artillery.

Because of the mud, trucks became useless, and soldiers and pack mules had to move the supplies. As Clark later said, "each hillside became a small but difficult military problem that could be solved only by careful preparation and almost inevitably by the spilling of blood." By 28 September the Fifth Army had made final preparations for the capture and occupation of Naples, where the Germans had recently punished the Neapolitans because of their anti-German uprisings during the invasion at Salerno. Colonel Darby and elements of the 82d Airborne Division, all under the leadership of General Ridgway, broke out onto the plain of Naples, while the British X Corps drove around both sides of Mount Vesuvius. After the final hills overlooking Naples had been captured, the dash to the city was rapid, and on 1 October the Allies made their entrance. Meanwhile, to the east on the other side of the peninsula, Montgomery's forces captured the valuable airfields around Foggia.

Naples, especially the port area, was in chaos, and one of the Fifth Army's immediate tasks was to get the city back on its feet. Key rail facilities had been wrecked, ships had been scuttled at their piers and in the harbor, and loading and unloading facilities had been demolished. In addition, the city was without water and power, and most of the sewerage facilities had been destroyed. In a 24-hour-a-day effort, American and British engineers began to rehabilitate the port and city. Within a week supplies were coming in steadily, and before long the port was handling thousands of tons of supplies daily.

Now that the Allies had captured Naples, the drive onward to Rome began. The basic directive given by the Combined Chiefs of Staff at the Trident conference had sent the Allies this far, and the principals at the Quadrant conference had added impetus by stressing the need to secure airfields at Rome. Even before Salerno, Rome was being seen as an objective by General Clark and others on the spot. And General George C. Marshall, U.S. Chief of Staff, though not a backer of the Italian campaign, felt that Rome should be taken as soon as possible. In early October both Alexander and Eisenhower expressed hope that Allied troops would be in Rome within a month. All fighting subsequent to Naples, said Eisenhower, "would have as its principal objective the pinning down of German forces far from the region of the major assault that was to take place the following year across the English Channel." The Allies, however, would have to do the job with what they had on hand, because the build-up for the cross-Channel attack took precedence. Thus, only 18 divisions would, even eventually, be available.

As for the Germans, at first the Allied commanders thought they would withdraw to the northern Apennine Mountains. Hitler himself considered doing just that in early October, pulling his divisions and corps back to a line drawn between Pisa and Ancona. Kesselring, however, did not advocate such a move. He felt that he could delay the Allies better, with fewer divisions, than could Field Marshal Rommel, commander in northern Italy, and although Hitler at first backed Rommel, the Führer gradually changed his mind. Accordingly, he sent Kesselring a message—which soon became Ultra intelligence—ordering him to hold a line south of Rome for as long as possible. Thus it was that Cassino, and its appendage, Anzio, would become certainties—the focal points of the battle for Italy during the winter months of 1943–1944.

General Omar Bradley once said that "in war there is no second prize for runner-up." A similar maxim must have been on the minds of the Allied planners, because there was no pause after Naples in the drive for Rome. German troops withdrew to the Volturno River line, but did so using strong delaying tactics. The Fifth Army followed—some 100,000 combat troops—with the British X Corps on the left along the fertile coastal plain and with the VI Corps on the right through more mountainous terrain. The 30 miles or so from Naples to the strongly defended Volturno was a struggle, made even more miserable by winter rains, chill winds and the ever present mud. Difficulties with the mud and water were so serious, in fact, that Clark postponed the Volturno River crossing until the night of 12–13 October. Then, with the X Corps—46th, 7th Armored and 56th Divisions—still on the left and the VI Corps—3d, 34th and 45th Divisions—still on the right, he ordered the two to attack simultaneously along the entire river line. In spite of difficulties, especially at the Triflisco Gap and at Capua where the Germans succeeded for a while in thwarting the crossings, the Fifth Army had secured its bridgeheads and had even forced the enemy back by nightfall of the 13th.

For the next month, as the Allied army advanced to the German Winter Line, a strong outpost to a formidable defense known as the Gustav Line, it suffered the worst weather and the most difficult terrain of the campaign. According to Clark, the "rain came in torrents, vehicles were mired above their hubcaps, the lowlands became seas of mud, and the German rear guard was cleverly entrenched." Fifth Army soldiers seemed to be engaging a major defensive position every day, but by the middle of November they were generally in position in front of the Winter Line.

Monte Camino was one of the most imposing of the peaks on the Winter Line. It had nearly been taken by a brigade of the 56th Division during the second week in November. Reinforcements at Monte Camino had suffered 60 percent casualties. Most of their officers were killed or wounded, for five nights they had only one day's rations, and during the entire fray the wounded had to be left on the cold ground without blankets. So severe were the conditions that General Clark ordered a withdrawal from the area. After that, the Fifth Army paused briefly for refitting and regrouping until the end of November.

Alexander was disappointed when he learned of the setback at Monte Camino, but he believed that even though it might later be harder than

At one point the Volturno River almost meets itself

ever to advance, it was better, perhaps, to wait. Although the 82d Airborne Division left late in November for England, other reinforcements came into the theater as the Fifth Army prepared for the final assault on this German defensive line.

Facing the Winter Line after the respite were three corps, the British X Corps on the left, the U.S. II Corps in the middle, and the VI Corps on the right, flanked by Montgomery's Eighth Army to the northeast. An early December move to capture Monte Camino and the peaks beyond, appropriately called Operation Raincoat, was deemed a success by 6 December, when the entire area south of Route 6, except Monte Lungo, came under Allied control. Monte Lungo was finally taken on the 16th, and after repeated attempts San Pietro Infine was captured on the 17th. The fall of San Pietro and the surrounding heights opened the way into the strategic Mignano Gap, but the Germans continued to hold the area north of Route 6 toward the town of Cassino. Progress for the next 30 days was meager and agonizing. With the capture in mid-January of Monte Trocchio (about a mile from the Rapido River), Fifth Army called the penetration of the Winter Line complete. This last advance, netting only about eight miles, brought General Clark's forces to the grim hills overlooking the soon-to-be-famous Gustav Line. Casualties had been high, nearly 15,000 for the Allies, and the units were exhausted. As the various commanders surveyed the hills beyond the Rapido they had no idea that come spring they would still be here, as well as at Anzio.

③. The Inevitability of Anzio

The course of the Allied campaign in the Mediterranean was shaped by events as they followed one another. In this regard, the decision to make a landing on the shores of Italy at Anzio was no exception. Many events made Anzio first a possibility and then a certainty, but the foremost factor was Hitler's decision to defend in southern Italy rather than in the north. When the Führer placed his confidence in Kesselring instead of Rommel, the major battles at the Rapido River and at Anzio became inevitable. What could have been simple skirmishes or delaying actions as the Allies made their way to Rome became events—major events—that drastically influenced Allied plans for defeating Germany.

As early as the end of October 1943, study and planning was being conducted for amphibious "end runs" that would cut behind and turn the German defenders in southern Italy. According to General Clark, these assaults presented many difficulties, and for one reason or another Fifth Army decided against them. But study continued at several echelons, and gradually the feeling grew that Anzio was the best place for such an operation. An assault at Anzio, or anywhere else for that matter, could only take place if enough shipping were available. Ships, however, were scarce in this theater, which had a low priority in a rapidly developing Allied global strategy.

On 3 November General Eisenhower met with his subordinates at the site of ancient Carthage, near Tunis and the Allied headquarters. Overall strategy in Italy was confirmed, including a Fifth Army amphibious assault in the Rome area. But this could only take place when the preponderance of the Fifth Army was in reasonable supporting distance of the beachhead—in the vicinity of Frosinone, some 30 miles northwest of Cassino. Since 68 Landing Ship Tanks (LSTs) were scheduled for transfer to England for use in Overlord, Eisenhower asked permission of the Combined Chiefs of Staff to retain them until 15 December. Keeping them, he said, would enable them to mount an amphibious assault that would speed the advance to Rome and its airfields. Otherwise, he explained, the Allies would have to continue their time-consuming frontal attacks. Three days later, the CCS gave their permission to retain the LSTs, thus making the amphibious operation possible.

On 8 November, Alexander issued orders which included an assault at Anzio (code-named Shingle), and Fifth Army headquarters began to lay plans. Only a relatively small force (one division) would make the landing to turn the enemy flank and enable the rest of the Allies to move quickly beyond Frosinone to link up with the beachhead units.

By mid-November both the Germans and the Italian winter had convinced the Americans and the British that it would be better to pause for a while and regroup. After that time only comparatively small advances were made by the Fifth Army, and highly placed Allied leaders were becoming impatient. Toward the end of November, Roosevelt and Churchill met at Cairo—they would later meet with Stalin—where they discussed the problem of keeping Overlord "in all its integrity" while still maintaining the Mediterranean as a theater "ablaze" with activity. The CCS had determined that facing the 14 divisions or equivalents the Allies would have in Italy by the end of December would be some 23 German divisions, 11 in the south and 12 in the north. This was a prospect which was not encouraging. Additionally, there was evidence that the Soviets were dissatisfied with the amount of Allied pressure being exerted in the Mediterranean and that Stalin favored an invasion of southern France to complement the cross-Channel attack. Churchill was also disappointed in the Italian campaign: for him Rome became the immediate and main Allied objective. With Rome in hand an advance could be made to the northern Apennines, where either the Balkans or southern France might be invaded. Until the time for such a decision became necessary, Churchill believed that Eisenhower's resources should be increased to accelerate this northerly advance. The main impetus could be given by extending further the 15 December deadline for the transfer of the LSTs to the United Kingdom.

When the Allies finally met with Stalin, they found that he favored the

Weather as well as the enemy holds up the Allies

southern France operation over continuing in Italy. In Italy, Stalin felt, the troops should go on the defensive if resources were not sufficient to sustain operations in both northern and southern France. Churchill was adamant in his belief that not to take Rome would be to acknowledge defeat, and argued for retention of enough assault shipping to make amphibious turning movements up the Italian peninsula. The American position was about the same as that of the British. The Allies decided to launch Overlord during May 1944, coupled with a secondary invasion in southern France. In a compromise decision the CCS agreed to postpone until 15 January the transfer of the 68 LSTs to England. Returning to Cairo, the Allied leaders named the southern France operation Anvil, and assumed that it would occur about the same time as Overlord. Meanwhile, it was hoped, the Allies, having captured Rome, would be in northern Italy at a line drawn between Pisa and Rimini.

The Shingle planning (involving only one division) begun in early November had been continued, but because of the slow Fifth Army advance it soon became apparent that there was no hope of getting to Frosinone or anywhere near it. General Truscott, whose 3d Infantry Division would be making the landing, believed that the basic Anzio strategy was sound, but agreed that the slow advance made a link-up within a month an impossibility. Truscott warned General Clark of this. The 3d Division, he said, "is perfectly willing to undertake the operation if we are ordered to do so and we will maintain ourselves to the last round of ammunition. But if we undertake it you are going to destroy the best damned division in the United States Army, for there will be no survivors." With the later inclusion of another division in the operation and the promise of more shipping, however, Truscott's fears vanished.

On 18 December, after a meeting with Eisenhower, Clark wired Alexander that the Anzio operation should not be carried out, both because shipping would not be available after the now twice-extended 15 January deadline and because Clark well knew that his troops would not be close enough to link up with the assault forces by the first week in January. The Fifth Army, he said, would continue to plan Shingle in the hope that landing craft would be available later on, as was his "urgent request."

Although Shingle seemed at this point to be relegated to the files—if not the wastebasket—two things happened that caused its resurrection. One was the conference at Cairo—heralded by the newspapers as concluding with complete Allied agreement on the scope and timing of future operations—which produced considerable change in the high command. The most important change was that General Eisenhower was appointed to direct the cross-Channel attack. During the first week in January 1944 he relinquished his command to Sir Henry Maitland Wilson, who had been his deputy. Overall leadership in the Mediterranean was now, therefore, British. General Montgomery, Eighth Army commander, was transferred to England to take over an army group, and was replaced by Lieutenant General Sir Oliver Leese. Lieutenant General Ira C. Eaker took charge as commander of the Allied air effort in the Mediterranean. Neither Alexander nor Clark was immediately affected by these command changes, but Clark did learn that he would, after the capture of Rome, take over Seventh Army and become responsible for Anvil. Important to the conduct of the Italian campaign was the fact that executive direction of the theater would, because Wilson was now at the helm, pass from the U.S. to the British Chiefs of Staff.

The second factor leading to the restoration of the Anzio operation was happenstance: Prime Minister Churchill became ill with pneumonia after Cairo, and was bedridden for a while at Carthage. Since he was so near Allied headquarters, Churchill began almost immediately to put his personal imprint on the Italian campaign.

Soon the plan for Anzio was brought out and dusted off, as the Prime Minister complained that "the stagnation of the whole campaign on the Italian front is becoming scandalous." By 23 December Churchill had decided that the "big amphibious operation" must become a reality, but both he and the other Allied leaders were aware that if it was going to happen the LSTs would have to be kept in the Mediterranean longer than was now authorized.

Portable pillbox dug out of the Gustav Line is removed to a rear area

At a meeting called by Churchill at Tunis on Christmas Day, Shingle came closer than ever to becoming a reality. Churchill, Eisenhower, Alexander, Wilson and others were present. The Prime Minister applied pressure to get Allied consensus on the staging of Anzio. Eisenhower, although he agreed to the need for continuing the advance in Italy, strongly argued that this landing would be risky and "would not by itself compel the withdrawal of the German front." Ike argued further that it would take a strong force and that a rapid build-up at Anzio would be difficult. There was no doubt that landing craft would be needed long after 15 January; hence Overlord, for which Eisenhower was now responsible, might be undermined. "The Prime Minister was nevertheless determined to carry out the proposed operation," wrote Eisenhower, who, after further warnings, agreed that the landing craft might be kept for another two weeks. Churchill then asked Roosevelt by message for approval to retain the LSTs until 5 February. Thus the Prime Minister had, as General Clark later wrote, "gotten back into the Mediterranean picture as a sort of super commander in chief, a role that he loved to play when the going was rough—and he did it very well." On this same day, 25 December, Alexander, who believed very strongly in Anzio, informed General Clark that a two-division Shingle was being planned. Three days later Roosevelt replied to Churchill that he agreed to postpone the transfer of the LSTs, but only if it did not affect the date set for Overlord.

Alexander came to see Clark on 27 December with more details about Shingle. The added division would be British, he said, because the venture was hazardous and heavy casualties might be expected. Both Allies should participate if the action was to be fierce. Clark, who was enthusiastic about the operation, assumed erroneously that the deadline for transfer of shipping had been abolished by Churchill in "his usual vigorous fashion." A few days later, Major General Alfred M. Gruenther, the Fifth Army chief of staff, attended a planning conference at Allied headquarters, where he found the consensus was that Shingle was not practicable and that it should be canceled because it would interfere with Anvil. Some of the top officers at the headquarters, said Gruenther, believed that Alexander was "badly off base" concerning Anzio. Then General Clark found out that the shipping would have to be released on 3 February. He was completely surprised that arrangements had not been made to retain the LSTs. "The number of craft available for Shingle," he said, and the limited time they would be available, rendered "resupply and reinforcement of the Shingle force impossible." Clark pointed out to Alexander that he had assumed that shipping was in fact available, since there had been no hint that it would not be.

At one point, General Clark said later, he felt that he had a pistol pointed at his head. Time for planning was becoming critically short, and he personally did not know how he would be able to do the job. But he said to his planning staff on 4 January, "We are supposed to go up there, dump two divisions ashore without resupply or reinforcement, and wait for the rest of the Fifth Army to show up. I am trying to find ways to do it, and am not looking for ways in which we cannot do it. We are going to do it successfully." General Clark again discussed the situation with Alexander, who cabled Churchill outlining the resources needed to do Shingle properly. Both he and Clark, said Alexander, were ready to accept any risk to do the job, but they must have additional resources. "Surely the prize is worth it," concluded Alexander, after warning the Prime Minister that Shingle would interfere to some extent with other planned amphibious operations, namely Anvil and Overlord.

Churchill agreed to try to secure enough craft for Anzio and, pending Roosevelt's approval, called a planning conference at Marrakesh, where he was now convalescing. Clark, who did not go to this meeting, warned his representatives not to permit the Prime Minister to "cajole" them into retreating an inch as far as shipping requirements were concerned. The discussions at Marrakesh lasted from the evening of the 6th to 8 January, and up until the last the possibility of Shingle's being approved for execution was in doubt. On the 8th, General Clark found out that Churchill "had forced through an arrangement assuring us of enough craft for resupply and . . . reinforcements." At the end of the meeting, Churchill wired Roosevelt that all responsible officers of both countries and all services agreed on the Anzio operation. "Everyone is in good heart and the resources seem sufficient," he added. "It should be possible to do this without conflicting with requirements of 'Overlord' and 'Anvil,' " and still be able to support the beachhead forces until the end of February. According to the official history,

> "All the problems were far from solved and the risks remained great, but Churchill had obtained at least 25 LSTs (the number deemed necessary by Clark) for the Anzio follow-up, he wanted the operation to be executed on 20 January, and there was high hope that the landing would get the Fifth Army to Rome in a hurry. When the word from Marrakech reached the Fifth Army headquarters, the atmosphere became jubilant: 'Operation SHINGLE is on.' "

During the time the decision for Anzio was being made, Allied planners from top to bottom were primarily concerned with a much larger situation, the overall campaign to destroy the Germans in southern Italy or at least to keep them pinned down so that they could not fight elsewhere. As plans for Shingle began to take shape, so did plans for an entirely renewed offensive—in concert with Anzio—along the Germans' closely held Gustav Line. Alexander's original concept of the Anzio landing was that the beachhead would be used as a stepping stone for a thrust northwest along the famed Via Appia, called Highway 7 by the military, into the Alban Hills—the Colli Laziali. While this was being carried out, the rest of the Allied forces would drive the enemy from the Liri Valley into a trap sprung by the amphibious troops who would then be straddling enemy escape routes in the Rome area. Clark saw these roles in reverse: the beachhead units would pin down some of the enemy forces, preventing them from helping in the defense of the Gustav Line and thus making the Allied thrust into the Liri Valley somewhat easier. Although Alexander's emphasis would later shift the beachhead objective to another town—Valmontone— his basic concept of trapping the Germans between the two forces remained unchanged. Clark, however, would eventually alter his own philosophy significantly.

Allied forces were to resume the offensive against the Gustav Line defenders a few days before Shingle was to be launched. The obstacles they faced, however, were formidable, in terms of both the terrain and the enemy. As General Clark wrote of the Rapido-Garigliano front, the terrain "was well worth noting . . . because it was studded with names that were to become familiar to Americans." The town of Cassino was one of these names, as was the monastery on Monte Cassino that overlooked it. The Rapido River was another, and so was the Liri Valley, soon to be named Purple Heart Valley by the Americans. For the concerted effort on two fronts that would be forthcoming in mid-January, the Liri Valley was without question the most important Fifth Army objective. This valley was the avenue by which General Lucas's isolated VI Corps, which would make the

Mediterranean operations hinged on the availability of landing craft

assault at Anzio, could be reached by the rest of the Allied forces. Just to open the door to the Liri would be a monumental task, for the valley sat in the middle of the most formidable Italian terrain and German defense system yet encountered. The Gustav Line was designed to make maximum use of the topography, which it did admirably, taking advantage of the swift rivers and rugged cliffs. Only a single water line faced the Fifth Army, but it was composed of three different rivers. The first, and fastest flowing, was the Rapido, which rose near Monte Santa Croce, coursed in a southerly direction about 15 miles past the town of Cassino and then beneath Highway 6, after which it became the Gari River. Then the Gari, a very short stream, intersected with the Liri. From this junction, at first south, then southwest to the sea, the river was called the Garigliano; it was about 15 miles long. The Rapido valley was the narrower of the two and was cut by numerous streams and canals. After it merged into that of the slower-moving Garigliano, the valley widened to about 12 miles as it approached the coast. During January, heavy rains and melting snow had turned these rivers into major obstacles. All had overflowed their banks, making quagmires of the lowlands. The situation was made even worse because the Germans had diverted portions of the Rapido purposely into the low areas to create swamps too soft to support Allied armor. Immediately to the northwest of the Rapido-Gari-Garigliano line were mountains—numerous

31

and rugged—with names like Monte Cassino and Monte Cairo. Also to the northwest were various towns, such as Minturno, Cassino, and Sant'Angelo and Sant'Ambrogio. The latter two guarded the mouth of the Liri River. The rivers and villages could be covered immediately by fire because numerous observation points and artillery sites were readily available, and effectively used, in the mountains behind.

The builders of the Gustav Line—the German Todt Organization—had left nothing to chance. They had created a carefully prepared defensive system that made the best use of dugouts, trenches, machine-gun emplacements, minefields, concrete bunkers, booby traps and barbed wire. Each of the villages became a strongpoint to be reckoned with. For example, according to General Clark the town of Cassino "was fortified as no other city" had been. "Heavy concrete and steel emplacements gave protection to enemy machine-gunners, and snipers and self-propelled guns and tanks guarded the approaches." To make matters worse, he said, near Sant'Angelo and elsewhere on the east bank of the river line lavish use was made of "mines concealed among the reeds and brush of the flat, marshy ground." Not only was the Gustav Line militarily sound in terms of engineering and terrain, but the entrenched enemy divisions were equal to the task ahead, ready for any attempt to crack Kesselring's defenses.

Monte Cassino guards the entrance to the Liri Valley

Facing the Fifth Army at the Gustav Line in mid-January were some 90,000 troops of the XIV Panzer Corps under the command of Generalleutnant (Major General) Fridolin von Senger und Etterlin. The LXXVI Panzer Corps, meanwhile, opposed the Eighth Army in a quiescent zone along the Sangro River from the crest of the Apennines to the Adriatic Sea. Both German corps were controlled by the Tenth Army, under General von Vietinghoff, and totaled some 150,000 soldiers. Held in reserve near Rome was the I Parachute Corps, controlled by Kesselring and his OB SÜD and numbering 24,000 men. Further, in northern Italy there were some 70,000 occupation troops belonging to the Fourteenth Army, under the command of Generaloberst (Colonel General) Eberhard von Mackensen, soon to become a prominent enemy figure at Anzio. Kesselring estimated in January that he needed eight divisions on the front, two in immediate reserve, two in reserve near Rome, and seven elsewhere in Italy, for a total of 19 divisions. With these, he reckoned, he could hold the line well into the summer, keeping the Allies completely bogged down.

During the several days before the capture of Monte Trocchio on 16 January, the impending renewal of operations to puncture the Gustav Line had added a sense of urgency along the front. As it was planned, the renewal was to be successful before the attack was launched across the beaches at Anzio. Thus there would be little rest for most of the Fifth Army units. In position at this time to make the assault against the German defensive line were seven Allied divisions. Two others were making preparations to land at Anzio within a matter of days.

Facing the northern portion of the river line was the French Expeditionary Corps (FEC), commanded by General Alphonse Juin. General Clark had known and respected Juin since his days in North Africa, and of him felt simply that "there never was a finer soldier." Two units were at this time under the control of the FEC. One was the 2d Moroccan Division, commanded by Major General André W. Dody. This division had arrived in Italy two months earlier and had already seen some action. The other was the 3d Algerian Division, with Major General Goisland de Monsabert in command. Arriving late in December, it too had seen action along the front. According to General Clark, both of the FEC division commanders were veteran and competent officers and the divisions were skilled in mountain warfare, a definite asset in this part of Italy. Of the French, correspondent Eric Sevareid said, "These men had a cold, implacable hatred of the enemy that was almost frightening; they were driven by such a fierce desire to show the world and regain their pride that one knew at once they would be stopped only by death and that in victory they would show no mercy."

The American II Corps, now commanded by Major General Geoffrey Keyes, was in line south of the French. Its 34th Division was located north of Route 6. The 36th Division, which had seen rough action almost continually since Salerno and was still commanded by General Walker, was in position south of the highway. Also located in the II Corps area was the 1st Special Service Force, a unique Canadian-American unit with special training.

Holding down the southern sector was the British X Corps, commanded by Lieutenant General Sir Richard L. McCreery, which also had been in the thick of the fighting since Salerno. Still assigned to this corps were the battle-tested 46th and 56th Divisions. Arriving on 17 January was the British 5th Division, which had come ashore at Calabria months earlier with General Montgomery's Eighth Army. A smaller unit assigned to the X Corps was the veteran 23d Armored Brigade.

The VI Corps of General Lucas, with the U.S. 3d Infantry Division and the British 1st Infantry Division, as well as several other smaller units, was not idle during this time. They were preparing—with a great deal of difficulty—for the invasion of Anzio. For reserves General Clark had the U.S. 45th Infantry Division and the 1st Armored Division. The former had been fighting from the beginning in Italy; the latter had not seen as much action simply because of the lack of opportunities to properly use an armored unit.

The Luftwaffe was only moderately active during January as General Clark began the Fifth Army's major drive into the Liri Valley. The first in the sequence of events at the river line was the crossing of the Garigliano in two places by General McCreery's X Corps. This was actually the third of a planned four-phase effort to crack the Gustav Line and advance through the Liri Valley for a link-up with VI Corps. The first and second phases had by this time already become history, the first being a successful advance by the FEC to face squarely the Germans along the upper reaches of the Gustav Line, and the second the capture by II Corps of Monte Trocchio. The fourth phase would be the hardest. On 20 January II Corps would deliver the crowning blow by crossing the Rapido south of Highway 6 and establishing a bridgehead near Sant'Angelo. Then it would move northwest, with maximum armor, up the Liri Valley to Frosinone. The II Corps's success, however, would depend on X Corps.

The plan for X Corps was to attack on 17 January with its three divisions—the 5th, 46th and 56th—and the armored brigade. The corps was to cross the Garigliano, advance on Minturno in the south and Sant'Ambrogio (one of the two villages guarding the mouth of the Liri River) in the north. Using boats because of the flood conditions, McCreery's men achieved surprise, contrary to his expectations, and the initial assault units on the left made their way across the river with relative ease. German resistance stiffened during the next two days. This was because the OB SÜD commander, Kesselring, decided immediately after the attack to commit his reserve to thwart what he considered to be a major breach of the Gustav Line. Beginning on the 19th, the I Parachute Corps and its 29th and

From the air the Liri valley resembles a jigsaw puzzle

90th Panzer Grenadier Divisions arrived from Rome in increasing numbers to help the embattled 94th Division contain the British advance. In spite of reinforcement by the enemy, the 5th Division had by 19 January seized Minturno; the 56th had consolidated its units and was holding a bridgehead almost two miles deep on the right flank of the 5th Division. At the other crossing site, across from Sant'Ambrogio, the going was much rougher. The swiftness of the river, the heavy fog and the German resistance combined to thwart the 46th Division crossing, leaving open the future left flank of II Corps.

McCreery's failure to take Sant'Ambrogio was a serious setback. General Clark felt that perhaps preparations for the Anzio landing—specifically, an unfortunate loss of DUKWs during the rehearsal—might well have contributed to the 46th Division's failure to take its objective. This was because the losses had to be replaced from craft belonging to X Corps, which, Clark said, "needed them badly during the Garigliano crossing." The failure would, McCreery thought, give the II Corps's 36th Division little chance for success when it attempted to cross the Rapido on the night of the 20th. Nevertheless, Clark maintained that it was essential to make the attack. He said he was "fully expecting heavy losses in order to hold all the troops on my front and draw more to it, thereby clearing the way for Shingle."

The II Corps's drive into the Liri Valley was to prove a disaster. It was a bloody time for the 36th Infantry Division, which was ordered again and again to attack. There were reasons for these desperate attempts to penetrate the Gustav Line. Political pressure was intense from the highest of Allied levels—especially Churchill—to capture Rome. General Clark said that not only did the Allies feel it politically necessary to take Rome, they had to retain the initiative so that the enemy would not remove his forces from the Mediterranean and use them in the defense of France. "Anzio consequently had become a vital part of that strategy; and to assure its success, it was essential that the Fifth Army exert the utmost pressure on the Gustav Line to prevent German divisions from being withdrawn and used to oppose the Anzio landings."

The pressure was just as strong on the German defenders. All soldiers had been read an order from Hitler which said in part that each and every man must "hold the Gustav Line to the very last." Then, too, Alexander had been very strong in his instructions to Fifth Army concerning the advance into the Liri Valley: "Make as strong a thrust as possible towards Cassino and Frosinone shortly prior to the [Anzio] assault landing to draw in enemy reserves which might be employed against the landing forces, and then . . . create a breach in his front through which every opportunity would be taken to link up rapidly with the seaborne operation." It was for these reasons that General Clark continued the attack—as did his corps commander, Major General Geoffrey Keyes—in spite of the British 46th Division's setback. Clark later wrote that "it was our mission to attack incessantly, and that's what we did."

Twelfth Air Force A-36s and P-40s flew 200 sorties on the 20th in support of the assault on the Rapido River. Following that, every artillery piece that could be mustered poured round after round into the same area—the vicinity of the battered village of Sant'Angelo. Several hours before midnight, two regiments of General Walker's 36th Infantry Division—the 141st on the north, the 143d just south—made ready to attack with all their strength. Each of the generals, from Clark to Keyes to Walker, was aware of the many difficulties the division would encounter. Since the Liri Valley was the most direct approach to Rome and Anzio, it had to be taken. Major General Ernest N. Harmon, the 1st Armored Division commander, believed that after the bridgehead was secure he would have little difficulty taking his tanks all the way to Frosinone. But General Walker became more and more concerned as time drew near for the attack. Although his superiors were never aware of his opposition to the mission, his diary reveals his thoughts. He wrote: "I'll swear I do not see how we can possibly succeed in crossing the river near Angelo when the stream [to the front of the village] is the MLR [main line of resistance] of the enemy." Even before the British 46th Division failed in its attempt to secure Sant'Ambrogio, General Keyes himself was somewhat pessimistic, telling

36

General Clark that the attack "risks becoming scarcely more than a . . . holding attack." When the 46th suffered its reversal, Keyes's warning was firmly underlined. To offset somewhat the lack of a secure II Corps left flank, the 46th Division was ordered to conduct a feint at Sant'Ambrogio on the night of the 20th, and a battalion from that division was attached to the 36th to follow and hold the left flank.

Engineering requirements for the assault were extensive. East bank minefields had to be eliminated and bridges had to be constructed and maintained, all under the most difficult conditions. Because the entire area was under constant German observation, it was impossible to place assault boats on the east bank during daylight, where they would be ready in advance. Instead, they had to be put in dumps at the base of Monte Trocchio. The assault troops would have to carry them several miles to the river line before they attempted the crossing.

Other factors, though seemingly minor, contributed to the debacle. After rehearsals at the Volturno by the 142d and 143d Regiments, the initial assault force, General Walker replaced the 142d with the 141st, simply to equalize combat time among units. Engineers would later say that this change broke up a trained infantry-engineer team. Accordingly, engineer and infantry coordination before the attack was in some cases almost nonexistent. Patrols seeking information about crossing sites and defenses were

U.S. 81-mm mortar in action during Rapido fighting

met with immediate opposition, and at times were unable to reconnoiter the west bank. German patrols were so active on the east bank that it was probable that they relaid some of the minefields cleared by the engineers.

Just before the attack, General Walker penned this note in his dairy, which summed up the situation as he saw it.

> Tonight the 36th Division will attempt to cross the Rapido River opposite Sant'-Angelo. Everything has been done that can be done to insure success. We might succeed but I do not see how we can. The mission assignment is poorly timed. The crossing is dominated by heights on both sides of the valley where German artillery observers are ready to bring down heavy artillery concentrations on our men. The river is the principal obstacle of the German main line of resistance. I do not know of a single case in military history where an attempt to cross a river that is incorporated into the main line of resistance has succeeded. So I am prepared for defeat. The mission should never have been assigned to any troops with flanks exposed. Clark sent me his best wishes; said he has worried about our success. I think he is worried over the fact that he made an unwise decision when he gave us the job of crossing the river under such adverse tactical conditions. However, if we get some breaks we may succeed.

Two hours before a foggy midnight on the 20th, the Americans launched their attack. They would not get the breaks General Walker had hoped for. In fact the opposite was the case. Nearly everything went wrong. The 141st Infantry Regiment, for example, found that many of their previously cached boats had been damaged by enemy artillery. With great difficulty the infantrymen carried to the river bank what boats were still intact. There they were taken immediately under fire by a heavy enemy artillery and mortar barrage. Boats and weapons were dropped as men went for cover. One company lost 30 men, including the commander and executive officer, during a single volley. When the troops scattered, they inadvertently wandered into the minefields. More men were killed and more boats damaged. Tapes marking passages through the minefields had become virtually invisible, having been trampled into the mud or destroyed during the rain of artillery and mortar fire. Half of the bridging equipment was lost before it ever got to the river, and by H-hour 25 percent of all the engineering assault equipment had been destroyed. Almost as fast as new equipment was carried to the assault positions it, too, was damaged or destroyed. In some cases, equipment was simply abandoned. One account of the 141st's attack lists on a full page the scores of things that went wrong: too few crossing sites, boats with unnoticed holes in them being put in the river simply to sink with their cargo, bodies of men blocking too narrow approaches, and infantrymen resenting taking orders from the engineers. These only were a few of the foul-ups. In spite of the almost overpowering difficulties, by 2100 a few boatloads of men had made it across the river, but behind them bridges were being destroyed as fast as they could be built. Using parts of other bridges, the engineers got one raised by 0400. By 0630 most of the 1st Battalion, using this one slippery bridge, was on the west bank of the Rapido and fighting for a toehold. At dawn one of the immediate problems was that the artificial smoke-generating equipment had, for various reasons, failed to arrive at the crossing sites. Without smoke a daylight attack to reinforce the beleaguered 1st Battalion was impossible, and the infantrymen on the west bank remained isolated for the day. That day, 21 January, was one they would never forget.

The 143d Infantry, below Sant'Angelo, fared little better. The engineers were able to guide one platoon of Company C, 1st Battalion, across the river exactly on time, but from then on the German reaction—intense artillery fire everywhere—caused havoc. Every boat in Companies B and C was destroyed, and casualties on both sides of the river were heavy. A footbridge was thrown up by the engineers, but it was destroyed soon after H-hour. Later, enough boats were brought forward by the engineers to get the rest of the casualty-ridden Company C across to the west bank. As daylight came and the small pockets of men came under German observation, their positions became untenable. Then German tanks came on the scene, whereupon the battalion commander ordered a withdrawal. (General Walker had ordered the battalion to hold on the west bank, but his order was received only after the withdrawal had been initiated.) Farther south the 3d Battalion lost all its boats, and under the impression that the engineers were bringing up more, merely waited. For various reasons, the battalion commander delayed the crossing. He was relieved of command by the regimental commander. But the command change was too late. No one got across the river.

For the next two days, as the assault along the beaches of Anzio was getting under way, the men of the 141st and 143d Regiments endured fierce enemy counterattacks and made repeated attempts to get relief to the tiny bridgeheads. The 36th Division, however, had butted headlong into one of the strongest defensive setups the Germans had ever constructed and manned in Italy. One officer was later quoted as saying, "I had 184 men . . . 48 hours later I had 17. If that's not mass murder, I don't know what is." Engineers continued their efforts to move more men and supplies over the river. Reinforcements did get across, in some cases, only to be decimated by enemy fire. A plan was laid on 22 January to have the 142d Regiment, the reserve for the division, relieve the remnants of the pinned-down 141st (by that time the 143d had completely withdrawn), but it was canceled when at about 2100 the same day 40 infantrymen of the 141st Regiment returned to the east bank. All the rest had been killed, wounded or captured.

The Fifth Army attempt to get across the Rapido has often been called one of the most colossal blunders of World War II. There were two sides to the picture. One was the desperate need to attack across the river to insure the success of the landing at Anzio and to facilitate the capture of Rome. The other was the feeling that such an operation was unnecessary, especially in the face of all the odds against success. After the war a Congressional board of inquiry investigated the entire effort, having been urged to do so by the Texas State Senate and the 36th Infantry Division Association of Texas, the 36th Division having been a Texas National Guard unit before the war, but the matter died when most of the witnesses proved to be ill informed.

After consideration of all the details, the Secretary of War found "that the action . . . was necessary . . . that General Clark . . . exercised sound judgment . . . ." Besides hearing criticism, the inquiry showed that "the river crossing was far from impossible, that the British just a few days before had staged a successful crossing of the Garigliano . . . and that the 34th Division successfully crossed the Rapido under equal if not more difficult conditions farther upstream a few days later." Fred Majdalany, writing about Cassino after the war, places the blame on the 36th Division, saying that the operation "was badly mishandled by the Command and Staff. It is difficult to see how he [Clark] could . . . be blamed for the execution of an operation that was . . . part of a larger design imposed on him from above. The operation was a difficult one, but not impossible." One thing is certain: the issue will never be settled. What seems clearer, however, is that General Clark erred when he selected the 36th Division to attempt the job.

B-26 bombs roads in the Liri valley

4. The Landing

By the time the Allied soldiers were sent to the beaches of the tiny resort town of Anzio, planning had been going on for months. Logistics plans, landing plans, loading plans, fire support plans, intelligence plans—all the myriad plans necessary for this amphibious landing, the most complex of military maneuvers, had been revised again and again until the chances for error had been reduced as close to zero as possible. The plans used by company and battalion commanders had all emanated from a broad mission given to the Fifth Army commander, General Clark, by the commander of the Allied ground forces in Italy, General Alexander.

Actually, Alexander's headquarters was not the ultimate source of the order; that was, and had been all along, Prime Minister Churchill. When on 9 January General Alexander went to the Fifth Army command post to talk with Clark and Lucas about Anzio, he brought along with him a message from Churchill that once again pushed for a quick capture of Rome, without which the Italian campaign will have "petered out ingloriously." Churchill was delighted, he said, with the approval for Shingle because he had felt for a long time that it was "the decisive way to approach Rome." Alexander also informed General Clark that the shipping problem had been cleared up and that D-day for the Anzio landing had been set for 22 January. If bad weather were to postpone the landing beyond 25 January, it would have to be canceled. After that date it would interfere with Overlord.

Alexander's formal instructions to Clark were spelled out in two quite general increments. The Fifth Army was "to carry out an assault landing on the beaches in the vicinity of Rome with the object of cutting the enemy lines of communication and threatening the rear of the German 14 Corps" (which was defending along the Gustav Line). Alexander amplified this in the second set of instructions: the objective of the landing was "to cut the enemy's main communications in the Colli Laziali (Alban Hills) area southeast of Rome, and to threaten the rear of the 14 German Corps." According to Alexander, the enemy would then be compelled to react to the threat to his rear: "[A]dvantage must be taken of this . . . to break through his main defences, and to ensure that the two forces join hands at the earliest possible moment." After all this, Alexander wanted the Fifth Army to "continue the advance north of Rome with the utmost possible speed." The Anzio orders were issued along with those concerning the Rapido River line, where the rest of the Fifth Army was to break into the Liri valley and link up with the beachhead forces. But as we have just seen, the Allied attempt to puncture the Gustav Line was brought to a quick and bloody standstill by the enemy and the terrain, before Anzio even got under way. So the landing across the beaches suddenly became a major operation far in the enemy rear.

Anzio beach area

Fifth Army orders had been completed and approved by 12 January. General Clark, who believed that he could not accurately predict the German reaction and who was not sure that the Gustav Line could be quickly breached, did not want to commit his troops to one unalterable course of action. Therefore he worded the Fifth Army and VI Corps mission statements very carefully. The task, as Clark saw it for Fifth Army, was to "launch attacks in the Anzio area." In his instructions to General Lucas he directed VI Corps: "a) to seize and secure a beachhead in the vicinity of Anzio. b) Advance on the Colli Laziali." Thus General Clark's translation of Alexander's orders left some freedom for independent action. VI Corps was supposed to establish a beachhead, but then would it advance *toward* the Alban Hills or *to* the Alban Hills? General Clark expected that if the enemy defended quickly at Anzio, as he had done at Salerno, VI Corps would have to assume defensive positions and hold on to the beachhead as well as possible. This was the course of German action that the Allies deemed probable, and there was to be a strong reserve force at hand to thwart any counterattacks. If no resistance was met, the words "advance to" the Colli Laziali would govern the operation, and VI Corps would then take whatever route was best, either Highway 6 or Highway 7. According to the official history, "whether VI Corps went on the defense or the offense after the landing would depend on how the corps commander, General Lucas, sized up the situation."

"Foxy Grandpa" was what Lucas's juniors called him, a nickname evoked by his appearance. According to General Truscott, he was a "lovable personality." Lucas, 54 and graying, seemed older than his actual years. He was born in West Virginia and had graduated from West Point in 1911. During World War I he had seen action as a battalion commander in France. In World War II, during 1942 and 1943, he had served as General Eisenhower's personal deputy for the campaigns in North Africa and Sicily. He had been assigned this job by General Marshall, who believed that Eisenhower would benefit from Lucas's maturity and good sense. When General Bradley left II Corps at the end of the Sicilian campaign, Lucas was chosen to take over. But only a month later Lucas assumed command of a more active unit, VI Corps, which he headed with competence in its advance up the Italian mainland. As for his being picked as commander of the invasion, his record made him a good choice. He was known not only for his sense of responsibility, but for his patience and experience. According to one source, everyone thought that if anyone could be successful at Anzio, it would be "Old Luke."

General Lucas himself was not so sure. His diary for the period is full of indications of doubt. He believed that he thought too often of his men and the conditions under which they fought; "I am," he wrote, "far too tenderhearted ever to be a success in my chosen profession."

Lucas's initial elation at the opportunity to "lead a vital and spectacular operation" gradually gave way to serious concern. As the time for the assault grew near, he became more aware of the risks involved. On 4 January he wrote in his diary that he was unenthusiastic because there was a lack of ships, troops and time: "Unless we can get what we want the operation becomes such a desperate undertaking that it should not, in my opinion, be attempted." A few days later General Alexander voiced his confidence in the VI Corps commander, but Lucas was not heartened. To Lucas, "this whole affair had a strong odor of Gallipoli and apparently the same amateur was still on the coach's bench." This was a reference to the Allies' disastrous Gallipoli campaign in World War I, in which many men were lost in a lengthy attempt to take the Dardanelles, split Turkey from her allies, and open an Allied route to Russia. The "amateur" was the First Lord of the Admiralty in 1915, Winston Churchill, one of the strongest proponents of the Gallipoli plan. Always the professional soldier who would do as his commanders bid, Lucas noted further: "These 'Battles of the Little Big Horn' aren't much fun and a failure now would ruin Clark, probably kill me, and certainly prolong the war."

After the conference on 9 January Lucas summarized both the event and his own forebodings:

"Apparently Shingle has become the most important operation in the present scheme of things. [Alexander] started the conference by stating that the operation would take place on January 22 with the troops as scheduled and that there would be no more discussion of these points. He quoted Mr. Churchill as saying, 'It will astonish the world,' and added 'It will certainly frighten Kesselring.' I feel like a lamb being led to the slaughter but thought I was entitled to one bleat so I registered a protest against the target date as it gave me too little time for rehearsal. . . . I was ruled down, as I knew I would be, many reasons being advanced as to the necessity for this speed. The real reasons cannot be military."

There was a note of optimism, though, hidden among the fears, as he continued:

"I have the bare minimum of ships and craft. . . . The force that can be gotten ashore in a hurry is weak and I haven't sufficient artillery to hold me over, but, on the other hand, I will have more air support than any similar operation ever had before. A week of fine weather at the proper time and I will make it."

General Lucas thought he detected too much optimism at the higher echelons. He did not see why the Germans could not hold the line both at

Major General
John P. Lucas

the Rapido and at Anzio. "Apparently everyone was in on the secret of the German intentions except me," he wrote, after having been told by a British admiral that by the time VI Corps reached Anzio the Germans would be north of Rome. He felt that perhaps the higher echelons were party to information about the enemy that he did not have. If the enemy did intend to retreat to Rome, all the more reason to strengthen VI Corps so that the Germans could be intercepted and destroyed. About the same time as the FEC was making its move on Fifth Army's right flank to face the Gustav Line, Lucas said in a note:

> "The general idea seems to be that the Germans are licked and fleeing in disorder and that nothing remains but to mop up. The only reason for such a belief is that we [the FEC] have recently been able to advance a few miles against them with comparative ease. The Hun has pulled back a bit but I haven't seen the desperate fighting I have during the last four months without learning something. We are not (repeat not) in Rome yet. They will end up by putting me ashore with inadequate forces and get me in a serious jam. Then, who will take the blame?"

There were a few who understood what was being asked of General Lucas. In private, while trying to tell Lucas of his confidence in him, Clark advised him not to stick his neck out as he (Clark) did at Salerno. General Patton, who had heard "the rumbles of the potential catastrophe" flew to Naples to bid his friend adieu and good luck. He said to Lucas, "John, there is no one in the Army I hate to see killed as much as you, but you can't get out of this alive. Of course, you might be badly wounded. No one *ever* blames a wounded general!" Turning to another officer, Patton told him, "Look here, if things get too tough, shoot the Old Man in the ass. But make sure you don't kill the old fellow!"

Eight days before the landing at Anzio, General Lucas turned 54, saying that he felt "every year of it." The corps commander sometimes appeared dejected, discouraged and tired; he was worried that his orders would send his men into "a desperate attack." According to one source, before the Anzio operation Lucas "seemed more impressed by its difficulties than by its opportunities."

Lucas's force grew considerably in size when the additional shipping was made available. Besides the two major units scheduled to make the assault—the U.S. 3d and the British 1st Infantry Divisions—the invasion force was augmented by the U.S. 504th and 509th Parachute Infantry Regiments, the 2d British Special Service Brigade with two Commando battalions, and the U.S. 6615th Ranger Force (Provisional), better known as Darby's Rangers. As was planned, there was a strong reserve. Immediately available to VI Corps was the 1st Armored Division, less Combat Command B; a regimental combat team from the U.S. 45th Infantry Division; and three additional battalions of artillery. If needed, the rest of the 45th Infantry and 1st Armored Divisions could be put onto the beachhead in short order. (For reserves in the Cassino area, General Clark had been promised two divisions from the Eighth Army, in whose zone action had not been brisk.) The Shingle force strength was expected eventually to total some 110,000 men; originally it was to have been only about 24,000.

Lucas's subordinate commanders had varied backgrounds, but all were highly experienced. The 3d Division commander, General Truscott, had been slogging up the Italian mainland with his men since just after the Salerno landings. Truscott was a Texan who was commissioned as a reserve officer in 1917, after which he served with the 7th Cavalry along the Mexican border. In 1942 General Marshall selected the then Colonel Truscott to head a group of American officers assigned to the Combined Operations headquarters in London—Lord Louis Mountbatten's staff. While based in England, Truscott participated in the Dieppe raid; later he was directly concerned with the organization of the first of the American Ranger battalions, with which he would once again be associated at Anzio. Truscott then went to North Africa where he filled higher-level staff jobs. Following that, in March 1943, he was named commander of the 3d Infantry Division.

Throughout his military career Truscott had earned the admiration of both subordinate and superior. General Lucas, for example, held the 3d Division commander in the highest regard, and Truscott's British colleagues all along the line respected him for his balance and judgment.

The other assault division commander, Major General William R. C. Penney of the British 1st Infantry Division, was a year younger than Truscott, having been born in 1896. Penney graduated from the Royal Military Academy, Woolwich, was commissioned in the Royal Engineers in 1914, and then served during World War I in France and Belgium. Before taking his 1st Division ashore at Anzio, Penney had led it in the capture of the island of Pantelleria, southwest of Sicily.

The two other divisions that would figure heavily, but not initially, at Anzio were the U.S. 1st Armored Division and the U.S. 45th Infantry Division. The armored division was commanded by Major General Ernest N. Harmon, who came from Lowell, Mass. Another West Point graduate, class of 1917, Harmon served in France during World War I and remained in Europe afterward, serving in the army of occupation. At North Africa he headed the 2d Armored Division, then took over as deputy commander, II Corps, during the Kasserine Pass battle. In the Tunisian campaign he was given command of the 1st Armored Division. The 45th Division was commanded by an Indiana man, another West Pointer, Major General William W. Eagles. A classmate of General Harmon, Eagles served in the United States during World War I. For all of the North African and Sicilian and half of the Italian campaigns he was assistant commander of the 3d Infantry Division. Taking command of the 45th in November 1943, he was to lead it until November 1944, when he was seriously wounded by a mine.

Colonel William O. Darby, the commander whom General Clark knew personally to be "an outstanding battle leader," had been with his Rangers since their organization in June 1942. General Truscott, however, was the one who actually got the Rangers going. While working in London, Truscott had been impressed by the British commandos and their training, and sought and obtained approval from General Marshall to organize a similar American unit. The name "commando," because it was already in use by the British, was not available, so reaching back into pre-Revolutionary American history, the Americans called for the name "Rangers" for what was to be a unique unit in the U.S. Army. According to General Marshall the Rangers were to be skilled in hit-and-run tactics and were to be trained in amphibious warfare. Truscott, who had known and respected the then Major Darby, had him assigned as the Rangers' first commander. At first the unit was only one battalion in size; later it grew to three. After overseeing the commando-supervised training in England, Darby and his Rangers had distinguished themselves in North Africa and at Salerno and Venafro. Then they were assigned to VI Corps for Anzio.

Colonel William O. Darby,
Rangers' commander

By this time in the Italian campaign, the Fifth Army chief, General Clark, had become an experienced wartime commander, having been at the job for five months under the most grueling conditions. A New Yorker and a West Pointer of the class of 1917, he had carried out assignments that had prepared him well for his army command. He had been a company commander in World War I. Between wars he had been assigned to the 3d Division and General McNair's staff. Before being appointed Fifth Army commander, he had been Deputy Commander in Chief for the Allied Forces in North Africa. One reason Clark knew General Juin so well was that before the invasion in North Africa he had taken part in a secret pre–cease-fire rendezvous with French leaders, including Juin.

General Clark's personality as a leader drew both criticism and praise; as with many things in wartime, there was an intense polarization of feelings—good and bad. General Clark himself realized that he probably appeared standoffish, but explained that "an army commander is a pretty lonesome fellow in combat. People don't come around to drop in on you." After the war subordinates would sometimes comment about Clark's arrogance. One of them said that the general's conceit was "wrapped around him like a halo." In *Rome Fell Today*, Robert Adleman and George Walton blame only the times, saying that "it seems as if the criticism of Mark Clark has taken on the aspect of a durable fad." Journalists who knew General Clark well thought highly of him, and disputed the "publicity conscious" charge that was so commonly reported.

Clark was especially concerned with the welfare of his men on the line, as was often demonstrated. But, although Clark knew his men, they did not know him. He was unsuccessful in getting the real warmth of his personality across to the rank-and-file soldier. Unfavorable stories about him could and did circulate rapidly because only a few of the tens of thousands of soldiers under his command could ever get to know him well enough to counter the tales. On the other hand, Clark's bravery was unquestioned. Once when he was observing the enemy at an exposed vantage point, oblivious to what were very real dangers, one soldier wondered aloud how "one son of a bitch [could] be so brave." Bill Mauldin once said of Clark,

> "I don't think you can make him out to be a great man, or anything of the sort. He was just a very human guy, doing the best he could. He had his limitations. But I think that a lot of the criticism of him occurred because he was associated with a bad time."

A middle-ground impression of General Clark was probably closest to being the true picture. Clark himself was well aware that he was sometimes wrong, and after the war summed up the entire situation.

> "I can't say I'm sorry about too much that happened in Italy, and I won't say that I ever felt sorry for myself that I had that particular spot. Frankly, I was grateful that I had been in the right place at the right time to get this high command. Of course, I realize it was a hell of a mission, sort of like being a guard on a football team while another guy gets the headlines for running ninety yards with the ball, but I don't mind. I had no false ideas about the Italian campaign, but I never bemoaned the fact that I was stuck with it. I was doing a job I wanted to do as well as I knew how."

The name Anzio meant different things to different people. To the natives, Anzio the town, together with nearby Nettuno, was a spa favored by early Roman emperors and still used as such by the Italians before the war. To the infantrymen and the generals Anzio the battlefield was considerably larger. That area was roughly defined by the shore of the Tyrrhenian Sea from the Moletta River to the Mussolini Canal, and inland by the towns of Aprilia, Campoleone, Carano and Cisterna.

Three main roads led from Anzio, spreading like fingers along and through the Roman plain which rose to the Alban Hills to the north and the Lipini Mountains to the northeast. Via Severiana followed the coast to the

Tiber River, but was not militarily significant. The Albano road (Via Anziate) went north out of town past Aprilia and Campoleone and eventually intersected Highway 7, the Appian Way, at the foot of the Alban Hills. The third road headed east out of town to Nettuno, then northeast to Cisterna where it, too, intersected Highway 7. These roads were paved, though few others in the area were, and of the three, the last two were the scene of intensive fighting during the months to come.

In the main battle area there were two distinct geographical entities. To the east and southeast was farmland that had been reclaimed from the ancient Pontine marshes. In the north and northwest were wooded areas and deep gullies.

The Pontine marsh area was drained by huge ditches, the object of one of Mussolini's public works projects. Otherwise untillable marshland had been converted into farmland, villages had been erected, and farmhouses—known as *podere*—dotted the region. Built of stone and thick-walled, each of these houses was easily converted into a strong fortress that could be readily defended by a few men with rifles and machine guns. Often it would take a tank in direct assault to overcome one, and even then the job was not an easy task. Flowing roughly from northeast to southwest, and emptied by pump into the sea, was the main drainage ditch, which with the West Branch, was called the Mussolini Canal. This obstacle—some 60 yards wide and 16 feet deep in places—was effective as a tank barrier.

The wooded and gullied area to the north and northeast was bisected by the Albano road and a railway. On the east side of the road was a reforested area known as the Padiglione Woods. To the west were denser woods called Selva di Nettuno, or Nettuno Wilds, a very apt description. The North African term "wadi" was used by the military to describe the country to the northeast, which was broken by deep ravines and narrow gullies carved roughly into volcanic soil. Many were tens of feet deep with sheer walls, and during the winter months they were filled with water that was hip-deep. Throughout the beachhead area the water table during the rainy season was high. Foxholes were often filled for days at a time, rendering them of little comfort during the cold winter months.

East of Anzio were two highways that led to Rome. The Appian Way (Highway 7), was the coastal highway connecting Rome with Naples. The Italians called the other highway Via Casilina; the Allied military called it Highway 6. Beginning north of the Volturno River as an offshoot of the Appian Way, Highway 6 wandered north and west through Cassino, the Liri Valley, Frosinone and Valmontone, then east of the Alban Hills, before entering Rome. Both highways were engineering masterpieces, with many cuts and fills; bridges across streams, rivers and glens; and embankments skirting swamps and lowlands. These two historic roads were to take on great importance in the battles to come.

The thousands of troops that were to take part in the landing at Anzio could only begin making preparations a few weeks before the event. Many landing and supply problems had to be solved, and extra care had to be taken to ensure that supplies would be available to the beachhead forces once they were ashore. Supply problems were compounded because two different divisions were involved—one American, one British. This necessitated two separate supply systems, since the Allies used different-caliber artillery and rifles, drove different vehicles and ate different food. One of the proposals turned down at the Marrakesh conference had been the suggestion that from the standpoint of supply it would be better to use only American divisions.

Two phenomena, both natural, made a January attempt to land at Anzio a hazardous undertaking. The first was the winter season, which promised rain, low clouds and high seas. Weather conditions in general could not help complicating the problems of supply over the beaches as well as of providing subsequent air support. The other problem was the beaches themselves. Not only were they much more shallow than those at Salerno, but two large offshore sandbars made it impossible for larger ships to get close to the shore. The Navy estimated that only smaller landing craft, such as Landing Craft, Vehicle and Personnel (LCVP) and Landing Craft, Assault (LCA), could get close in to the beaches.

To lessen the effect of bad weather the assault convoy was loaded so that all its contents could be put ashore within two days. To enable larger boats to unload over the shallow beaches, mobile piers were devised. In spite of disapproval of the procedure by the conferees at Marrakesh, the Fifth Army staff devised a unique procedure to increase the amount of supplies unloaded across the Anzio beach. Two-and-a-half-ton trucks were overloaded at Naples, then backed into the LSTs. After they reached the beaches at Anzio, the trucks would simply be driven off and dispatched immediately to the supply dumps. Each LST had been "spread-loaded" in Naples with Class I (food), Class III (fuels) and Class V (ammunition) supplies, so that the loss of an entire ship would not seriously reduce supplies in any particular category. Each truck carried only one class, so that it needed to go to only one dump in Naples and one dump in Anzio. As soon as the LSTs were unloaded, empty trucks, which had been standing by, would be driven back on board the craft head first, after which they would be returned to Naples.

The biggest preinvasion problem facing VI Corps was that of a rehearsal for General Truscott's 3d Division, which had not recently undergone amphibious training. Brought up along with the subject of preloaded trucks at the Marrakesh conference, rehearsals were flatly declared by the Prime Minister to be a waste of time. Churchill maintained that "all troops [were] trained troops and needed no rehearsal." In spite of the American argument that many of the men were recent replacements, the Prime Minister continued his opposition, insisting that "one experienced

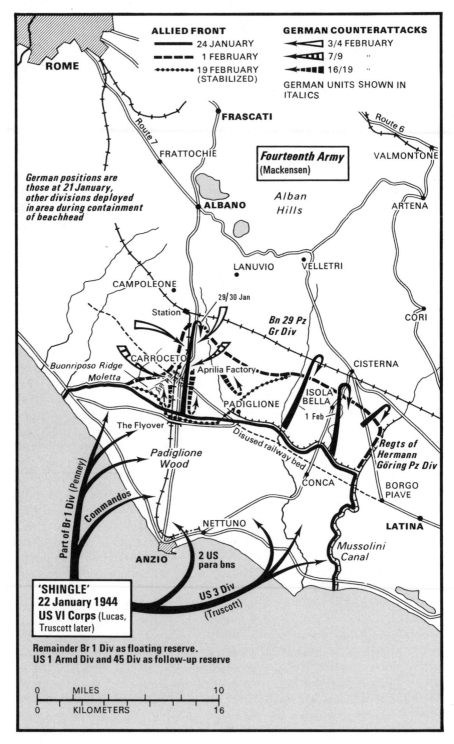

OPERATION SHINGLE

officer or non-commissioned officer in a platoon [is] sufficient." U.S. Fifth Army representatives prevailed, however, and a rehearsal was scheduled. General Clark, himself a staunch believer in the value of a rehearsal, later wrote that "it was only with the greatest difficulty that we managed time for a rehearsal of the Anzio landing."

Generals Lucas and Truscott were the officers who really pressed for the rehearsal. In the time since the 3d Division's initial training in the United States, and its earlier landings, there had been so many divisional replacements that amphibious expertise was sorely lacking. Truscott believed, too, that rehearsals were even more important for the naval component of the invasion, writing that "Mr. Churchill to the contrary, full scale rehearsal is the only way in which . . . understanding [between Navy and Army] can be tested."

Lucas and Truscott, who feared the worst, saw their fears realized. The rehearsal was not only bad, it was nearly fatal to the whole Anzio operation. Operation Webfoot, as the event was called, got under way on 18 January when the rehearsal ships, commanded by Rear Admiral Frank W. Lowry, USN, attempted to put the 3d Division ashore on practice beaches at Salerno at 0200. Truscott, who was aboard a headquarters ship,

Major General
Lucian K. Truscott

was unable to observe what happened, but after getting ashore at daybreak he began to get the bad news. The initial battalions had gone inland toward their objectives, but with considerable confusion. Since they had been disembarked too far out, few units were put ashore at the right place, and everyone arrived late. By 0800 not one tank or artillery piece had made it to the beach, yet tanks and guns were supposed to have gone in almost concurrently with the infantry.

The worst news was yet to come, however, as Truscott began to get reports of a real disaster. In the darkness a navigational error had caused the LSTs to open their doors far from shore. There the smaller DUKWs were discharged, carrying their precious cargoes of artillery. Heavy seas were much too rough for the tiny vessels and many were swamped; the final tally showed that the 3d Division lost 43 DUKWs; nineteen 105-mm howitzers with fire-control equipment; and several antitank guns. By mid-morning the "beaches were in chaotic condition, and the whole landing plan was completely disrupted." Appended to the formal report given Clark by Truscott was the crisp summation: "To land this division on Anzio beaches as it was landed during this rehearsal would be to invite disaster if the enemy should counterattack at daylight with forty or fifty tanks. In my opinion there is grave need for additional training." General Clark soon called Truscott to his headquarters, where, with report in hand, he informed the 3d Division commander: "Well, Lucian, I've got your report here, and it's bad. But you won't get another rehearsal. The date has been set at the very highest level."

Admiral Lowry also was dejected by the experience and by the realization that there was no time for another try. General Clark had placed the blame on the Navy, where the trouble seemed to be an appalling and "overwhelming mismanagement." Clark contacted Lowry and arranged a meeting between Navy experts and Lucas and Truscott. General Lucas, reporting to Clark after the meeting, told the Fifth Army commander that he believed everything had been done to make the actual landing a success. Lowry himself had assured Truscott that the "Navy would do its utmost to set matters straight, and to put us ashore exactly as we wished." As it turned out, Lowry made good on his promise.

The fleet of two task forces put to sea with its cargo of invaders early on 21 January. About this same time the Allies along the Gustav Line were undergoing their tribulations. The U.S. 36th Division was being forced to abandon its precarious hold on the west bank of the Rapido River. When the renewed Allied effort to crack the line had begun on 17 January, Field Marshal Kesselring had quickly decided to reinforce the German defenses with his Rome area reserves, the I Parachute Corps and its 29th and 90th Panzer Grenadier Divisions. Soldiers from these units had been arriving along the southern part of the Gustav Line since the 19th to stiffen the defense against the British X Corps, which had managed to secure a

British X Corps troops shuttle ambulances across the Garigliano

bridgehead across the Garigliano River. In the meantime the 15th Panzer Grenadier Division, considered by the XIV Panzer Corps commander, General Senger, as the finest he had, was holding off the 36th Division with little difficulty. German units in the Anzio area, however, were almost nonexistent; only a few engineer units from the 29th Panzers, the bulk of which had just been sent to the Gustav Line, remained in the Anzio-Nettuno area.

General Alexander's intelligence section had stated, correctly, that before the assault against the river line there were two German divisions in reserve near Rome (the 29th and the 90th). Fifth Army G-2 (intelligence) personnel were more pessimistic, believing that there were also some paratroopers and armored forces nearby, and that the German reaction to any assault at Anzio would be violent. Fred Sheehan, in *Anzio, Epic of Bravery,* writes that it would have been impossible for the Allies to have known quickly enough that the Germans had withdrawn most of the 29th Division to the Gustav Line defenses, leaving only the few engineers behind. This may well not have been the case. British intelligence officials, armed with Ultra information, were aware just before Shingle got under way of the weakened German defenses near Anzio. According to the British, an assault across the beaches could not be countered with German reinforcements inside of 48 hours. For some reason, however, this information was either never received or never used by the Fifth Army. Up until the moment the Allies set foot on the Latium beaches everyone expected bitter opposition.

When General Lucas got on board the USS *Biscayne,* his headquarters ship for the landing, he was not as despairing as he had been earlier. He wrote that he had many misgivings, but that he was also optimistic. If good weather continued for several days, he said, "I should be all right." Lucas believed that thus far the amphibious operation was undiscovered by the enemy, and that the invaders had "a good chance of making a killing." But he still feared the overoptimism of the higher commanders. His cautious approach had been supported by two events. One happened on the day Clark's G-3 (operations officer) delivered the Fifth Army orders for Anzio. The G-3 explained to Lucas about their "vague" wording, saying that the VI Corps mission was "to seize and secure a beachhead," and that that was all that was expected. A great deal of thought had gone into the wording of the orders so that Lucas would not feel compelled to push on to the Alban Hills at the risk of his corps. If it were possible to advance to the hills, however, Lucas was free to do so. The other event was the cancellation of a plan to air-drop the 504th Parachute Infantry Regiment 10 miles north of the resort town. Had that move been made, VI Corps would have been required to push north to effect a link-up, but with its cancellation the incentive to quickly expand the beachhead in that direction was removed.

Rear Admiral Lowry's Task Force 81 was responsible for getting the ground forces ashore and for their support afterward until the beachhead was well established. To carry out his mission, Lowry divided his force into

Bearers carry men wounded on January 22 at the Rapido

two, Task Force X-ray to take the Americans in, and Task Force Peter to do the same for the British. Five cruisers, 22 destroyers and a host of lesser ships escorted the troop-and-equipment-carrying boats. Minesweepers, rocket-launching ships, gunboats, submarine chasers and repair ships were all on hand to perform their specialized tasks in support of the assault.

To help ensure the permanency of the beachhead, Lieutenant General Ira C. Eaker's Mediterranean Allied Air Force (MAAF) weeks before the landing bombarded the Italian railway system steadily to isolate the Anzio area so that it could not be reinforced by the Germans. On the 16th, this effort was intensified. All in all between 1 and 22 January the tactical Twelfth Air Force and the strategic Fifteenth Air Force dropped more than 5,400 tons of bombs on lines of communication in the area.

Because the Fifth Army wanted to achieve surprise, there was no preliminary bombardment of the beaches before the infantry landed. To the north, as a ruse, another naval task force was assigned the job of bombarding the town of Civitavecchia and carrying out fake landings. The only preinvasion action at Anzio was to be a short but intense rocket barrage, launched from landing craft fitted with multiple rocket launchers.

Termed a "motley fleet" by the British historian Eric Linklater, the 243 vessels must have nevertheless been a formidable force as they steamed north at about five knots, skirting enemy mines and making a course calculated to deceive the enemy as to the exact location of the landing. The 21st was a bright sunny day, and detection by the Germans was feared, but the Air Force had knocked out the Luftwaffe reconnaissance base at Perugia and the Allies enjoyed virtual command of the air. Not an enemy plane was sighted. Men of VI Corps lolled on the decks, slept, checked their equipment and discussed with some concern what they might find when they set foot on land.

General Lucas's landing plan called for his 40,000 men to make three separate assaults. Peter Beach was about six miles north of Anzio. There the British would make their move with the two battalions of the 2d Special Service Brigade—the 9th and the 43d Commandos—on the right flank and the 2d Brigade Group of the 1st Division on the left. The center assault group, across X-ray Yellow Beach next to the port of Anzio, was to consist of Darby's three Ranger battalions, the 509th Parachute Infantry Battalion and the 83d Chemical Battalion. Four miles to the east, using X-ray Red and Green beaches, General Truscott was to take the whole 3d Division ashore at once with three regiments abreast.

General Penney's 1st Division and the two Commandos had two objectives. They were supposed to move quickly inland from Peter Beach through the wadis to the Moletta River on the extreme north. They were also to cut the Anzio-Albano road to the east. Darby's Rangers and the 509th had the job of capturing the port facilities and silencing any coastal defenses which might oppose the landing. This mission called for speed, because the port was needed as quickly as possible to facilitate unloading of supplies and equipment. Truscott's men were to advance north and east to set up roadblocks along the Cisterna-Anzio road, establish bridgeheads across the Astura River and capture the bridges spanning the Mussolini Canal. All of the assault forces were then to consolidate a beachhead centered on the port of Anzio.

Since strong defensive action and subsequent fierce counterattacks were expected, the Allied plan called for a powerful reserve force. The bulk of the 1st Division, including an attached regiment, was to remain aboard its shipping to serve as a floating reserve. The 504th Parachute Regiment, landing behind the 3d Division, was also a corps reserve. In accordance with the belief that there would be considerable enemy opposition, Lucas placed emphasis on digging in early once the initial objectives were reached.

Just after midnight on 22 January the assault vessels dropped their anchors; landing craft slipped into the water, and patrol vessels herded them into formation. Admiral Lowry had made good his promise, because in nearly perfect unison the first wave was heading shoreward a few minutes before 0200, the scheduled time to land. The only noise the Allies heard was the five-minute barrage of rockets that was rained on the objectives just before H-hour. Even when the infantrymen stepped ashore there was nothing but silence and darkness. It was incredible! What everyone had deemed to be an impossibility had come true—the landing was virtually unopposed and the Germans were taken unawares. General Lucas, in the command ship *Biscayne* about 3½ miles offshore, was unable to believe his eyes as he stood on the bridge and saw "no machine gun or other fire on the beach." In short order Lucas wired General Clark "PARIS-BORDEAUX-TURIN-TANGIERS-BARI-ALBANY," which meant "Weather clear, sea calm, little wind, our presence not discovered. Landings in progress. No reports from landings yet."

Although the Germans were taken by surprise that January morning, they did not waste any time before reacting. Field Marshal Kesselring implemented Case Richard, his plan for meeting an emergency in Italy. Because of his shortage of troops in the Anzio area, Kesselring's intelligence estimates credited the Allies with a good chance for quick success. If VI Corps reached Valmontone and cut Tenth Army's lines of communication, if it turned upon the rear of Tenth Army, or if it simply established a strong base, Kesselring would have to order a withdrawal from the Gustav Line. The OB SÜD commander was not about to let any of this happen, and by 0500 had ordered the 4th Parachute Division, just then being activated near Rome, and several replacement units of the Hermann Göring Division to block the roads from Anzio to the Colli Laziali. When he reported the Allied assault to the German high command he asked for reinforcements, and the 715th Division from France and the

D-day at Anzio: Fifth Army GIs wade ashore

114th Division from the Balkans were ordered to Italy. Kesselring was also ordered to activate a new division from several lesser units in northern Italy; it was to be called the 92d Division. Colonel General von Mackensen, commander of the Fourteenth Army was ordered by Kesselring to send reinforcements, and by nightfall the 65th Division from Genoa (minus one regiment), the 362d Division from Rimini (also minus a regiment), and elements of the newly formed 16th SS Panzer Grenadier Division from Leghorn were all on their way to the Anzio area. All this had been done before 0730, after which Kesselring "reluctantly" told Vietinghoff to transfer what he could to Anzio. The Tenth Army commander chose to dispatch immediately the just-arrived I Parachute Corps headquarters, the 3d Panzer Grenadier Division (less one regiment), the 71st Division and portions of the Hermann Göring Division. Later in the evening, Vietinghoff ordered the 26th Panzer Grenadier Division and parts of the 1st Parachute Division to withdraw from the Adriatic front and head for Anzio. Kesselring's last move—about 0800—was to order the commandant of Rome to rush down to the Anzio area and take command until the I Parachute Corps headquarters could arrive on the scene. In a little over six hours Kesselring had caused all or parts of 11 different divisions to begin converging on Anzio, and by late afternoon of the 22d the first reinforcements began to arrive. The phrase "unopposed landing" was soon to fall into disuse around Anzio.

5. Progress and Problems

One of the main reasons the beaches at Anzio were dark and silent when the Allies landed was the intensity of the action along the Gustav Line, which the Germans were making every effort to hold. American newspapers announced the landing as a spectacular event. A headline in the New York *Times* on Sunday, 23 January, spoke not only of the assault but of a final objective for the Allies: "ALLIED UNITS LAND BEHIND NAZIS IN ITALY, 16 MILES FROM ROME." The article went on to talk about the landing as "the most stunning and hazardous operation of the Italian campaign."

In the center of the beach at Anzio—X-ray Yellow—stood a big white casino, the immediate objective of the Rangers. The building had been spotted much earlier in aerial photographs of the area, and Colonel Darby, the Ranger commander, had jokingly told the Navy planners that when he got out of the LCI he did not want to have to look to the right or left. "I'll be moving so fast," he said, "that I want to make sure that . . . I will run right through the front door of the casino." Admiral Lowry's sailors almost did it: Darby missed by only 10 or 20 yards. What was more important when the Rangers landed was that no one was shooting in their direction. The Rangers' plan called for the 1st and 4th Battalions to land abreast, the 1st on the left. The Ranger 3d Battalion and the 509th Parachute In-

Anzio and Nettuno

fantry Battalion were to follow in successive waves, but using the same landing craft. This irregularity had caused Darby some worry, because he disliked not landing his entire force at once, and it was yet another reason why the Rangers were glad that there was no opposition.

Resistance in town and at the port was, at worst, negligible. There was a little scattered shooting, and at dawn in the 1st Battalion sector a German personnel carrier was captured, its two occupants having been shot and killed. The 3d Battalion overran a battery of coastal defense guns, and the 4th Battalion had no difficulty in taking care of a few Germans who were guarding a footbridge near the railroad. By dawn the Rangers had taken Anzio and carved what they called a "good beachhead." In the meantime, the 509th had charged down the coastal road and captured the town of Nettuno. Behind the Rangers and the 509th came the men of the 504th Parachute Infantry Regiment. One infantryman later remarked that "the day was sunny and warm, making it very hard to believe that a war was going on and that we were in the middle of it."

The British under General Penney at Peter Beach fared about the same. About the only things that slowed them down were a few mines and the shallow water. General Alexander, in an early message to Churchill

61

regarding progress, said, "We appear to have got almost complete surprise. I have stressed the use of strong-hitting mobile patrols . . ." But mobile patrols were impossible in the wadi country that slashed part of the British sector, though by midday the British had formed a perimeter about two miles deep. The commandos made a swing to the right, cut the Anzio-Albano road and established a roadblock just north of Anzio.

General Clark, just before a visit to the Anzio beach with General Alexander, received another message from Lucas: "NO ANGELS YET CUTIE CLAUDETTE"; this meant that there were no German tanks yet and the 1st and 3d Division attacks were going well. The 3d Division *was* moving in quickly. By mid-morning its troops were three miles inland, and all its tanks and artillery had been brought ashore. Not only that, but the bridges across the Mussolini Canal were in 3d Division hands and had even been prepared for demolition. By dark the 30th Infantry Regiment had taken the crossings over the West Branch, from Padiglione eastward. According to General Truscott, the previous poor performance on the part of the Navy had put the sailors on their mettle. This time, he said, "our Navy comrades gave us one [landing] which was almost unbelievably smooth and accurate." About the only action seen by Truscott's division was the capture of some 200 men from the 29th Panzers; most of them were still in bed when surprised by the American infantrymen. Bill Mauldin spoke of another engagement. "Among the first German prisoners captured," he wrote, ". . . were several drunken German officers who had driven a Volkswagen into the gaping doors of an LST. They must have had a terrible hangover when they woke . . ."

The worst German harrassment of the day came from air raids that occurred every few hours and forced everyone to take cover, thus wasting valuable time. After the assault waves had gone ashore, engineers cleared remaining minefields, graded roads across the dunes and handled streams of men and supplies coming ashore. Even though a minesweeper was damaged by a mine and bombs sank an LCI, the port at Anzio was opened by midafternoon. The shallowness of Peter Beach slowed down the British unloading to such a degree that General Lucas shifted that operation to the Anzio port. As the 22d came to a close, VI Corps had put ashore 36,000 men, 3,200 vehicles and most of its initial supplies—about 90 percent of the personnel and equipment of the assault convoys.

Fighters and bombers of the MAAF gave maximum support to the assault on D-day, flying more than 1,200 sorties against varied targets. Spitfires and P-40s during the first day were able to shoot down at least seven Luftwaffe planes while damaging several others. Only three Allied planes were lost. For most of the day, American and British aircraft flew patrols over the beaches—Spitfires at high altitudes, P-40s lower—to stifle enemy air interference. A similar defensive pattern was repeated on the 23d and 24th, except that more emphasis was given to bombing targets on the defense perimeter before taking up the patrols, and to strafing troops and vehicles before returning to base. Concurrently, medium bombers hit roads and junctions behind the beachhead, and heavier bombers attacked lines of communication around Florence and Rome and in the Liri Valley in a continuing effort to isolate the battlefield.

The first of the German reinforcements began to trickle in on the 22d. I Parachute Corps and its commander arrived around 1700 to take over command of the tactical situation from the commandant of Rome. Elements of the 3d and 29th Panzer Grenadier Divisions and the 71st and Hermann Göring Divisions were on hand before the day was over. They were placed on the line to form a tenuous defense. Field Marshal Kesselring was feeling somewhat more optimistic at the end of the day, because, as he said later, the

> "Allies on the first day of the landing did not conform to the German High Command's expectations. Instead of moving northward with the first wave to seize the Alban Mountains . . . the landing forces limited their objective. Their initial action was to occupy a small beachhead. . . . As the Allied forces made no preparations for a large-scale attack on the first day . . . [we] estimated that . . . [they] would improve their positions, and bring up more troops. . . . During this time sufficient German troops would arrive to prevent an Allied breakthrough."

B-17s taxi at Allied Foggia airfield

The OB SÜD commander felt confident enough in the situation late in the day to disapprove a recommendation by Vietinghoff to withdraw from the Gustav Line; instead, he ordered the Tenth Army commander to stand fast.

The 3d Division was destined to see some bitter action before dawn the next day. Newly arrived elements of the Hermann Göring Division were the source of the difficulty for General Truscott's cavalry troop, which had seized and was holding the bridges over the main Mussolini Canal, including one west of Sessano. The cavalry commander, Major Bob Crandall, went to see Truscott at his headquarters, where he received the sage advice to be particularly alert at night for any German reaction. It was almost a year before Truscott saw Crandall again. Several hours after darkness fell, tankers from the Hermann Göring Division hit the cavalry and 29th Division soldiers attacked 30th Infantry positions along the West Branch. The Germans recaptured the bridges along the West Branch and the one near Sessano.

Later on, Major Crandall decided to check on his men at the Sessano bridge, and drove headlong into the middle of the Germans who now held it. The major was immediately captured. Early on the 23d the Germans pressed their attack in the 30th Regiment's sector, moving as far southeast as La Ferriere, where they destroyed the bridge just as a 3d Division battalion arrived. Before the day had ended, 30th Regiment infantrymen regained their positions across the West Branch, but only after sizable losses.

D+1 (the following day) saw advances too. By the end of the day the Allied perimeter had been doubled. The front began at the Moletta River on the left flank, extended west to east along a line north of the Padiglione Woods, continued eastward above the towns of Campomorto, La Ferriere and Conca, then ran along the West Branch to the Mussolini Canal itself. From the junction of the two canals, the Allies controlled the main canal to the sea. The boundary point between the two divisions was an overpass on the Albano-Anzio road. The British portion of the front extended seven miles, while the American part was about 21 miles long. All the while, reserves of both forces were built up, as corps artillery, corps and division transportation units, the 36th Engineer Regiment and mountains of supplies were unloaded from the Liberty ships and the LSTs.

Action on the 24th and 25th was more intense than it had been on the 23d. German resistance stiffened, as reinforcements began to arrive in ever greater numbers. On the 24th both Allied divisions probed to the north. The intermediate objectives of VI Corps were the road centers of Campoleone, for the 1st Division, and Cisterna, for the 3d. These two villages had to be captured to secure positions from which to launch new attacks from the beachhead or to use as strongpoints in a defense if it became necessary. Minor changes were made in the units on the front line and in the re-

General Clark (with field glasses) heads toward Anzio on D-day

serves. The 504th Parachute Infantry was relieved from corps reserve and assigned to the 3d Division. General Truscott sent it to secure the right flank of the corps, along the Mussolini Canal, where it replaced Major Crandall's 3d Reconnaissance Troop. Darby's Rangers took the place of a 3d Division regiment, the 7th Infantry, on the division's left flank. The 2d Special Service Brigade was withdrawn from Anzio and transferred to the British X Corps at Cassino, and the first contingent of the U.S. 45th Division, the 179th Regimental Combat Team, arrived at the port where it was placed in reserve.

On this same day, the 24th, General Penney launched a mobile patrol up the Anzio-Albano road; it surprised a German outpost at Carroceto and continued northward almost to Campoleone. On the 25th, exploiting what seemed to be an enemy weakness, the 1st Division made a limited attack with one brigade, a squadron of tanks and some artillery to seize Aprilia, a group of brick buildings dubbed the "Factory" by the Allies because of their precise layout. Aprilia, however, had been occupied by fresh German troops the night before, and the fighting was sharp. Nevertheless, the British drove through a minefield, took the town and captured more than 100 prisoners. The next day the 29th Panzers, who were apparently sensitive to Allied occupation of this strongpoint, tried in vain to retake the Factory with an entire regiment. This attempt cost the Panzers four tanks and another 46 prisoners. By 28 January the 24th Guards Brigade of the 1st

65

Division had moved still farther north, about a mile and a half from the Factory, where it stopped to regroup for a push on Campoleone.

Meanwhile, in the 3d Division sector the 15th and 30th Regiments attacked on the 25th with a battalion each, but made no progress toward Cisterna. After reorganizing a bit, the regiments renewed their efforts on the 26th, this time supported by tanks and the total firepower of division artillery. The advance was still limited, and the fighting proved to be bitter and intense. General Truscott at this point proposed to the VI Corps commander that the 45th Division's 179th Regiment and part of the 1st Division relieve the 3d Division on line so that it could mount an all-out attack against Cisterna. General Lucas was not yet ready, Truscott wrote later, because he wished to wait until parts of the 1st Armored Division arrived during the next day or so. After another attempt to push on to Cisterna on the 27th, the 3d Division broke off the attack to prepare for a larger VI Corps effort which was to take place on the 30th.

While the Allied forces were preparing for the forthcoming offensive, an American GI, Technician Fifth Grade Eric G. Gibson, was conducting his own. Assigned to the 3d Division as a company cook, he along with other replacements was rushed into the battle for an enemy strongpoint. Gibson led his squad against four enemy positions and secured the left flank of his company. Keeping several yards ahead of his men, Gibson drew enemy fire, then attacked the enemy position, firing all the while. Ignoring artillery and submachine-gun fire, Gibson continued to advance, killing and capturing several enemy soldiers. Ordering his squad to lay down a base of fire, he crawled 125 yards through an artillery concentration to attack and capture another emplacement. Reconnoitering a ditch ahead of his squad, Gibson attacked yet another German strongpoint. His squad heard the exchange of fire and, moving forward, found that Gibson had killed one more German soldier but had himself been killed in the fighting. Sergeant Gibson became the first man to receive the Medal of Honor in the Anzio campaign.

Although Kesselring at first had doubts about the ability of his meager forces to stand up against any sort of Allied move toward Rome, they soon became allayed. For the first two days, unknown to VI Corps, the roads to Rome were essentially open to a quick Allied advance. By the 24th, German defenses were strong enough that the high command no longer feared an Allied breakthrough in that direction. General Siegfried Westphal, Kesselring's chief of staff, wrote later:

> "At the moment of the landing south of Rome, apart from certain coastal batteries standing by, there were only two battalions . . . [T]here was nothing else in the neighborhood which could be thrown against the enemy on the same day. The road to Rome was open. No one could have stopped a bold advance- guard entering the Holy City. The breath-taking situation continued for the first two days after the landing."

Since no attack had been made on the Alban Hills on either the 23d or 24th, wrote Kesselring, "the first and greatest crisis had been overcome." On the 24th OB SÜD decided to order General von Mackensen's Fourteenth Army headquarters from Verona to take command of the defense at Anzio, because I Parachute Corps was not equipped to handle the many units that were now in the area. General von Mackensen assumed command of the Anzio front on the 25th. At this point there were parts of eight German divisions in the vicinity of the beachhead, and elements of five more were en route.

Mackensen was then ordered by Kesselring to launch a "decisive" counterattack as soon as possible to eliminate the beachhead so that Vietinghoff's divisions could be returned to the Gustav Line. By the 28th, the Fourteenth Army had developed a plan to strike across the entire front on 2 February. Vietinghoff proposed to use the 65th Division opposite the British sector, the 3d Panzer Grenadiers in the center and the Hermann Göring Division in front of Truscott's 3d. Before this attack could be carried out, however, Lucas's VI Corps would make a move of its own.

General Lucas's main interest, initially, was building up the port and the beachhead to sustain the almost 100,000 men that would eventually be at Anzio. He was concerned about having enough supplies and equipment because he feared that the Germans could establish supply lines on land faster than he could by sea. Information from his G-2 that Kesselring was sending troops to Anzio from the Gustav Line bolstered this cautious stance. Thus Lucas allowed his forces to increase so that he could keep the

German fire ignites an LCI at the beachhead

Anzio's town square after American bombing attacks

corps intact even under the worst possible conditions. Despite the success so far, the VI Corps commander was still not happy. Of the total situation at this point, Lucas wrote in his diary, "The strain of a thing like this is a terrible burden. Who the hell wants to be a general?" By the 25th, however, Lucas believed that the beachhead was relatively safe and that he could now plan for future operations, because men, supplies and equipment were indeed rolling in. In spite of heavy gales during two days of the first week, LSTs were unloading 1,500 tons of supplies a day, mostly ammunition. There were about 40 LSTs on the "ferry run" from Naples to Anzio, as well as an array of Liberty ships lying offshore, discharging their cargo onto lighters of every description. By the 29th, VI Corps had put nearly 70,000 men, 500 artillery pieces, 240 tanks and 27,000 tons of supplies on the beaches. General Lucas personally supervised some of the logistical jobs, such as organizing the masses of supplies and equipment that were cluttering the beaches.

The hesitation by VI Corps during those first days at Anzio, together with later revelations that the road to Rome was at first wide open, raised questions that have been argued about ever since. But in the beginning Alexander and Clark were not concerned, although some of the infantrymen on the scene were. In one British battalion, for example, officers and men often discussed the subject. There were no Germans, they said, so what was stopping the division? Since by the 25th Generals Alexander and Clark had displayed no dissatisfaction with the accomplishments of VI Corps, Lucas thought that everything was all right. The two Allied leaders visited Anzio often. So, Lucas said on one occasion when he was talking with General Keyes, they had had "plenty of opportunity" to tell him that they were dissatisfied with his progress, if in fact they were.

At this time, however, neither opponent knew what the other was doing. The Allies especially were not party to the detailed movements and plans of the Germans. But one Italian observer, Admiral Franco Maugeri, wrote later that by the 25th it was plain that "the Anglo-Americans had once more missed the bus." Starting on that morning he saw German unit after unit going to the Anzio area. There were long columns of 88-mm guns, howitzers, larger self-propelled guns, Tiger tanks and armored cars. There were medical units, field hospitals and battalion aid stations. "The Nazis were digging in at Anzio," the admiral added. "They were going to make a fight of it." According to Adleman and Walton, Lucas had tried to

"hedge a bet while taking a calculated risk. As a result, he was forced, until the day he died, to undergo a flood of armchair strategy which explained over and over again that if he had possessed only a bit of audacity, he could have cannonaded his force directly into undefended Rome."

On the 25th Alexander paid VI Corps another visit, still expressing satisfaction with the situation. By the 27th, however, unknown to Lucas, Alexander was complaining to Clark that VI Corps was not being aggressive enough. That same day, however, Lucas was meeting with his division commanders concerning future plans. He now felt that within a couple of days VI Corps would be strong enough to push on. Clark, too, had become increasingly concerned with the caution that Lucas had so far exhibited. As early as the 23d, Clark had noted in his diary, "Lucas must be aggressive. He must take some chances. He must use the 3d Division to push out." On the 25th Clark actually urged minor offensive moves, and by the 28th he was impelled to tell Lucas to "speed up [the] advance toward Cisterna." That same night Lucas felt obliged to sum up his thoughts about it all.

Apparently some of the higher levels think I have not advanced with maximum speed. I think more has been accomplished than anyone had a right to expect. This venture was always a desperate one and I could never see much chance for it to succeed, if success means driving the German north of Rome. The one factor that has allowed us to get established ashore has been the port of Anzio. Without it our situation by this time would have been desperate with little chance of a build-up to adequate strength.

Had I been able to rush to the high ground around Albano and Velletri immediately upon landing, nothing would have been accomplished except to weaken my force by that amount because the troops sent, being completely beyond supporting distance, would have been immediately destroyed. The only thing to do was what I did. Get a proper beachhead and prepare to hold it. Keep the enemy off balance by a constant advance against him by small units, not committing anything as large as a division . . . until everything was set. Then make a coordinated attack to defeat the enemy and seize the objective. Follow this by exploitation.

This is what I have been doing but I had to have the troops to do it with.

General Lucas planned to launch his main attack on the 29th, but had to delay it for a day because General Penney and General Harmon, the 1st Armored Division commander, who had just arrived with two-thirds of his division, were not quite ready. The plan finally decided upon, on 27 January when Lucas met with his commanders, was straightforward in concept. The 1st Division, together with Combat Command A of Harmon's division, would make the main attack. This was to be a 1st Division drive up the Albano road to Campoleone, at which point Harmon's tanks would pass through the British and after a wide swing attack the Alban Hills from the west. Meanwhile, for the secondary attack, the 3d Division, the Rangers and the 504th were to capture Cisterna, cut Highway 7 and advance toward Velletri.

U.S. engineers remove explosive charges planted by the Germans

Just before Lucas's attack, the Luftwaffe stepped up its activity. German bomber groups had been deployed to the area from Greece and northern Italy, and on the 29th they struck twice with fury—the heaviest attacks so far. At sundown the Luftwaffe pulverized the beachhead, aided by 88- and 170-mm artillery, and sank a Liberty ship and a British cruiser, HMS *Spartan*. Part of the problem for Allied air defense, though it was not always critical, was that the Luftwaffe operated from nearby bases, while Allied aircraft had to fly all the way from Naples. Since planes could only take off and land during daylight, there was a short period at dawn and dusk when American and British planes had either not yet reached Anzio or, at the end of the day, had started back to base. Not only that, but the Germans were able to spend a longer time over the battlefield, since they did not use as much fuel getting there. On the daily raids, however, the Luftwaffe usually lost several aircraft, because Allied fighters, together with the 40- and 90-mm aircraft guns that had been set up to protect the beachhead, constituted a fairly efficient defense. During the first 10 days at Anzio, Twelfth Air Force fighters flew some 450 sorties a day; 65 enemy planes were shot down against the loss of fewer than 20 by the Allies. For the most part, British and American aircraft enjoyed command of the air, and for a few days were even able to set up a fighter strip at Nettuno. This strip had to be abandoned, however, because it was within artillery range of the enemy, who began to destroy the Spitfires on the ground.

On 29 January, Lucas assured Clark that VI Corps was ready to attack. "We will go all out tomorrow or at once," he said, "if conditions warrant." The VI Corps commander made some last-minute changes in Allied dispositions, putting the 36th Engineer Regiment on the corps left flank, along the Moletta River, and placing the 179th Regimental Combat Team on the right, replacing the 504th at the Mussolini Canal so it could take part in the advance against Cisterna.

The British attack was relatively successful, in spite of the fact that Kesselring and Mackensen, in preparing to carry out their plan to strike on 2 February, had concentrated their troops along the same avenue of approach that the British were going to use. This German force, commanded by Major General Fritz Graeser and called Combat Group Graeser, consisted of 17 infantry battalions with heavy artillery support. As the British got under way, the Fourteenth Army was in the process of massing its own troops. Just before midnight on the 29th, General Penney's 1st Scots and 1st Irish Guards, in a preliminary thrust to secure the line of departure (abbreviated LD) for the main British attack, tried to take some crossroads about 2,000 yards south of the Campoleone railway overpass (flyover, the British called it).

Heading north, the 1st Scots Guards on the right hit a heavily mined roadblock, then pushed on through with severe losses. The 1st Irish on the left met even worse opposition, in the form of enemy tanks and self-propelled guns, and were soon forced back. The threat of enemy armor worried Lucas, so he took a battalion from the soon-to-be-attacking 1st Armored Division and sent it to help the British. In what turned out to be a sharp battle, British and American tanks finally turned back the German armor and the Irish were able to get back to their forward positions. Not until 1500 on 30 January—because of the fierce fighting it had taken just to get to the LD—did the British get under way for the main attack. The 1st Battalion, King's Shropshire Light Infantry, and the 1st Battalion, Duke of Wellington's Regiment, drove northward and took one objective—the high ground just south of the overpass at Campoleone. British tanks were taking on enemy antitank guns beyond the railroad as it began to get dark, and they were unable to move any farther north. Both the infantry and the tankers called off the battle for the night.

Perpendicular to the Albano road was an old railway bed, going northwest out of Carroceto station, that General Harmon planned to use as an LD. First, however, the 1st Armored Division would have to secure it, just as the British had to do with their LD. Given the task of clearing the old railway was the commander of Combat Command A, Colonel Kent C. Lambert, who tried a well-armed reconnaissance-in-force tactic to accomplish the job. Turning left off the Albano road, the expedition made its move around noon on the 29th. The American tanks were at first stopped far short of their goal by minefields. Intense enemy fire, where there was supposed to be only a thin German defense, added to the tankers' difficulties. Colonel Lambert withdrew out of range of the accurate German fire, and then halted his tanks. There they became hopelessly mired in the soft mud considerably short of the railway embankment, and there they waited out the night while they were reinforced by more armor from the division.

On 30 January, a cold, cloudy day, the men of the 1st Armored Division tried once again to clear the old railway bed. After the stuck tanks were freed, five armored companies moved forward, only to get bogged down once again in the soft ground as they engaged the enemy. General Harmon then dispatched the 6th Armored Infantry to attack astride the railway. Although the armored infantry managed to advance somewhat through "a wall of mortar and machine gun fire," by the end of the day they were still struggling to secure the 1st Armored Division's LD. The British, meanwhile, had not yet taken Campoleone, although they had secured the approaches to the overpass.

Because of the difficulty experienced by the 1st Armored Division, General Lucas changed the attack plan. Instead of advancing north from the railway bed to the left of the 1st Division, the tankers were to wait until the British infantry had captured a road junction at Osteriaccia, about half a mile north of Campoleone. Then General Harmon's armor was to pass through the 1st Division and attack up the Albano road; the British were to follow as soon as possible. While all this was going on, the 6th Armored In-

Twelfth Air Force A-20 bombs German positions at Cisterna

fantry was to continue its attack to secure the 2½ miles of old railway bed that had been the 1st Division LD.

Not until 1030 on the 31st did the British get under way in their move to take the Osteriaccia road junction. They finally made their way across the railroad leading northwest to Rome out of Campoleone station, but that was as far as they could go. The Albano road from there to Osteriaccia was, as someone said, a "hornet's nest of resistance" with tanks and self-propelled guns covering every conceivable route north. In some cases, the German tanks had actually driven through the rear of buildings and were using the front windows as firing ports. Minefields made the defenses even stronger. The British 3d Brigade could make no progress and decided to withdraw to allow armor to take care of the strong German defenses.

Then the British decided to renew the advance north around noon, and in a prelude launched an armored attack up the Albano road. When the lead battalion reached the railway with its medium tanks, it too was forced to a standstill by intense enemy fire of all descriptions. The 1st Division's artillery was brought to bear, massing fires on the enemy positions; then the British attacked again. The Germans refused to budge. With small arms, mortars and self-propelled guns, some as close as 300 yards to the embankment, they beat off the British attack.

To prepare for his own newly assigned armor attack, General Harmon on 31 January sent an armored battalion to reconnoiter the ground west of the Albano road for possible ways to cross the railway to Rome. At one point the battalion encountered well-entrenched enemy machine gunners, overran them and took the ridge they had been holding. The Germans soon counterattacked, but were beaten off with losses of about 175 men. Another ridge was taken in similar fashion, and the light tanks then moved into position along the railroad. Here they were stopped quickly by anti-tank guns and heavy artillery. Having no chance of forcing their way across the railroad before dark, the reconnaissance force withdrew.

The 1st Armored Division's 6th Armored Infantry was doing no better in its attempt to secure the old LD along the abandoned railway. The attack got under way early—about dawn—but ran headlong into machine gun fire from firmly entrenched weapons. Minefields to the front were covered by fire, making for a well-coordinated defense. Armored support was late in coming to the assistance of the men on foot, and, heavily shelled by enemy artillery, the infantrymen were able to move only about a quarter of a mile. The 6th Armored's commander finally reported to General Harmon that further advance was impossible. The regiment was withdrawn and was relieved by the 24th Guards Brigade. That night General Lucas placed the 1st Armored Division back into corps reserve.

Thus it was that the VI Corps main attack failed to take its objectives, although it had gained considerable ground against an enemy that had been pushed almost to the breaking point. The British 1st Division, with the

Campoleone station—a key point in the British sector

help of the American 1st Armored, did reach Campoleone, and had actually penetrated the German main lines west of the Albano road. A two-mile gap, soon to become known as the Campoleone salient, had been made between the defending 65th Infantry and the 3d Panzer Grenadier Division. On the right flank of VI Corps, however, the situation was considerably more grim.

Two battalions of Darby's Rangers—about 750 men—led the 3d Division attack at 0130 on 30 January. Within half a day—12 hours—only six Rangers would be left. The rest would be either dead or in German hands. The plan was for the 1st and 3d Battalions to move out an hour before the main attack and infiltrate in the darkness—unseen by the Germans—to Cisterna, take the town by surprise and hold it till the main body of the division arrived. At 0200, the 7th and 15th Infantry were to conduct the main effort. The 7th Regiment on the left, after having passed through the 30th Infantry, which was holding the front line, was to move northeast to take Highway 7 north of Cisterna. The 15th Regiment planned to follow the Rangers, then cut Highway 7 south of town. As a diversion, the 504th Parachute Infantry would attack along the Mussolini Canal. According to General Truscott, the one-day delay requested by General Penney and General Harmon in activating the VI Corps plan was unfortunate for the

75

Rangers as well as for the 3d Division. During the night of the 29th, unknown to Allied intelligence, the Germans had relieved parts of the Hermann Göring Division with fresh troops of the 26th Panzer Grenadier Division that had just arrived from the Eighth Army front. Instead of one division, as expected, the 3d encountered two divisions, both fully capable of conducting a strong defense.

The Rangers were half an hour late in getting off; they were supposed to leave at 0100. Both battalions made their way silently—each man with extra ammunition and hand grenades—in columns along a narrow ditch that cut through the fields to the right of the road between Conca and Cisterna. The men could see German positions on either side of the ditch, but on this cloudy and moonless night the Rangers were, it seemed, undetected by the enemy. By dawn the lead Ranger was coming out of the ditch at a point where it intersected the Cisterna-Conca road. Only 800 yards lay between him and Cisterna. But now the Germans opened up. Against the head of the column a contingent led by three self-propelled guns laid down a devastating blanket of fire. Darby's men deployed quickly and soon destroyed the three guns, but as the light increased, enemy weapons of every description began to take their toll. The Germans were all around, concealed in houses and haystacks and anything else that offered cover, and with machine guns, mortars and sniper fire they systematically picked off the Rangers one by one. The Americans had been caught without cover or concealment and more men were lost as they scrambled and crawled for ditches or unoccupied farmhouses. During the first few hours the Rangers fought an intense pitched battle. Finally, at 0730, the 1st Battalion broke radio silence to report its precarious position. By 0830 a few of Darby's men had made it to the Cisterna railway station at the edge of town, but most of them remained pinned down in the flat and coverless fields.

A battalion of the 15th Infantry, together with the 4th Ranger Battalion, followed as scheduled about an hour after the Rangers had left. They were never able to relieve the 1st and 3d Battalions. At the village of Isola Bella the 4th Battalion was stopped by enemy machine gun fire coming from various *podere* south of town. The battalion commander and his men tried to outflank these strongpoints, but the process took hours. By dawn the 4th Battalion was still far from Cisterna and the enemy was still close by. For the rest of the day these Rangers were pinned fast by the Germans; two strong attempts to make a breakout had failed. Increasingly, men were being killed or wounded.

All through the morning the 1st and 3d Ranger Battalions fought the entrenched Germans, but about noon the end was near. German tanks had come into Cisterna via Highway 7 and had begun to race back and forth through the remaining Ranger positions. Since they had no antitank guns, the Rangers had to engage the armor with what they had—grenades and bazookas. One tank rumbled into a spot occupied by a handful of men commanded by Sergeant Thomas Fergan, who quickly jabbed a "sticky" grenade onto it. Another of his men hit the tank with a bazooka round, and a third Ranger finished it off by climbing on board and dropping a grenade down a hatch. But the Rangers were simply no match for the tanks, and the few men that remained tried to withdraw. According to the official history,

"at 1230, 1st Sergeant Robert E. Ehalt of the 3d Battalion sent a final message from the battalion command post. Only ten men were left . . . [H]e was out of contact with all the companies, and he was destroying his radio as the tanks approached. Of the 767 men in the Ranger attack only six escaped. Most of the men were captured by the Germans."

As it turned out, the German main line of resistance was in front of Cisterna, not behind the town as was expected, and thus the Rangers were not the only Americans to run into trouble on the 30th. The 3d Battalion, 15th Infantry, was scheduled to follow the Ranger 4th Battalion, but when the 4th was stopped, the 3d was unable to launch its attack. General Truscott then directed the 3d to follow the route of the 1st and the 3d Ranger Battalions to try to effect a relief. But then, after the Rangers surrendered, the 3d Battalion's orders were again changed. Now it had to turn and attack Isola Bella from the rear, which it did. In a morning of fierce fighting, clearing houses one by one, the 3d Battalion captured the village. Meanwhile the 1st Battalion, 15th Infantry, was moving with some difficulty along the 3d Battalion's right flank, but finally it too gained its objective. During the process the tank company leading the attack destroyed a Mark IV tank, overran three 75-mm antitank guns and rounded up what was left of two demoralized companies of the Hermann Göring Division.

The northeastern axis of the 3d Division attack, along the left of the road to Cisterna to cut Highway 7 above town, also made little progress. The 1st Battalion, 7th Regiment, unable to make a ground reconnaissance because the 30th Infantry was still fighting for the 1st Battalion's line of departure, found that what the men had thought were hedgerows were actually drainage ditches overgrown with briers. These 20-foot-wide ditches could not immediately be crossed by supporting armor. Even without tanks the 1st Battalion pressed on, but the troops were soon caught in the open when German flares lit the area. "All around the enemy opened fire," says an account, and in the full light of day the scene was worse than it had been at dawn. The Germans occupied high ground on three sides of the battalion and poured automatic weapons fire into its ranks. Despite heavy casualties, including the battalion commander, about 250 men managed to infiltrate to one of the higher knolls which had been cleared of Germans only with difficulty. Later, tanks were able to come forward to support the exhausted GIs, and the 1st Battalion was able to hold its ground.

The 2d Battalion, 7th Regiment, was held up in its attempt to go directly up the Isola Bella–Cisterna road. The cause of the delay was simply the intensity of smoke from artillery fire that had been laid down by support units. When the battalion finally left the LD, it was immediately taken under fire by a unit of the German 1st Parachute Division, which had dug in only the night before. The American attack stalled, but with the support of the reserve battalion it was tried again in the afternoon. With Sherman tanks and M-10 tank destroyers in support, weapons that "systematically demolished each German-held farmhouse and haystack barring the way," the infantry by the end of the day had reached its objective, a knoll about halfway to Cisterna.

The diversionary attack of the 504th—a move along the Mussolini Canal to destroy two bridges north of its junction with the West Branch, and then to cut Highway 7—was somewhat more successful. Just before the infantrymen reached the bridges, however, the Germans blew up both of them. A number of prisoners were captured as the 504th moved onto Highway 7, but by this time the Germans had also blown the bridges across Cisterna Creek. Since the supporting armor could not cross the creek to help the infantry, and since the Germans sent in the 7th Luftwaffe Jäger Battalion to strike the rear of the 504th, Cisterna Creek was as far as

Men of the 504th Parachute Infantry Regiment cross the Mussolini Canal the 504th could advance. The Jäger Battalion was a particularly tough unit made up of Luftwaffe disciplinary offenders who chose to fight as infantry in preference to serving terms in prison.

The 3d Infantry Division had gained only about a mile and a half by late afternoon on 30 January. Later in the evening the division mopped up remaining pockets in the rear and dug in for the night. The enemy remained active, however, counterattacking and probing for weak points. One position near Isola Bella was occupied by Sergeant Truman Olson and a weary crew who had just completed a 16-hour assault during which a third of their company had been killed or wounded. Placed forward with the unit's only machine gun, the men were supposed to ward off the counterattacks that were expected. During the hours of darkness, Olson's crew was killed or wounded one by one as the Germans kept up incessant and accurate fire. At dawn, already wounded once and now the only man remaining with the machine gun, Olson met the full force of a 200-man German counterattack. For half an hour the gallant, mortally wounded infantry sergeant kept the enemy at bay. Then he was hit again. Refusing evacuation, he kept on shooting for another 90 minutes, killing 20 more enemy soldiers. The Germans were forced to withdraw. Olson was posthumously awarded the Medal of Honor for his bravery and incredible determination.

The next day General Truscott modified somewhat the 3d Division plan of attack. Instead of simply cutting Highway 7 north and south of Cisterna, the 7th and 15th Regiments were to attack along the Ponte Rotto and Isola Bella roads, which converged on Cisterna. Before the attack all available supporting artillery was used to pound the strong German positions, but a planned B-26 air strike had to be called off because of low clouds.

The 1st Battalion, 30th Infantry, was brought up from division reserve to lead the 7th Infantry attack northeast up the road from Ponte Rotto. Even before this battalion could clear its LD at Ponte Rotto, 14 German tanks attacked from Cisterna. But this time the tables were turned. The German tanks, deploying to meet the Americans, were unable to maneuver effectively in the soggy fields on either side of the road. Five German tanks were disabled, and the rest of the armored force hurriedly withdrew. In spite of this success, however, the 1st Battalion was able to make only about 500 yards before darkness set in.

On the extreme left flank of the division, 7th Regiment's 1st Battalion, which on the 30th had held the knoll against strong German counterattacks, again tried to cut Highway 7 north of Cisterna. The battalion moved with relative ease forward to the railroad, surprising and capturing about 150 Germans who had not yet dug in to meet an Allied attack. But along the railway the situation changed quickly. The 1st Battalion had run headlong into the German main lines. Seeing that his men were unable to advance farther and were smothered by intense German counterfire, the battalion commander, Major Frank Sinsal, withdrew the unit some 400 yards to a reverse slope. During the night the infantry drove off counterattack after counterattack. Major Sinsal and about 100 men—no longer in touch with the various companies and nearly out of ammunition—were barely able to hold through the night until reinforced.

On the morning of the 31st the battered 4th Ranger Battalion forced its way to Isola Bella, where it joined the 15th Infantry Regiment, having the day before finally cleared the Germans from its path. Behind smoke laid down by Allied aircraft and the 82d Chemical Battalion, the 15th Infantry made its move shortly after noon. Its 2d Battalion, which had not seen action the day before, began to advance up the Isola Bella–Cisterna road, preceded by intense and massed artillery fire. Cisterna was only two miles away, but the Germans fought back with everything available, and by nightfall the infantry had gained only about a mile. Meanwhile, the regiment's 1st and 3d Battalions were having troubles of their own as they tried to first fight their way easterly to the Littoria-Cisterna road. Both battalions were counterattacked sharply in the process, and for the 3d Battalion the situation became critical. Three of its four tank destroyers—vehicles mounting 3-inch guns—were almost immediately put out of action, and the Germans threatened to break through the battalion's ranks. Only a last-ditch effort by Sergeant W. E. Nesmith and his remaining M10 saved the Americans. Nesmith was able to ward off the armor-assisted counterattack almost by himself. As this was happening, the Germans who had struck out at the 1st Battalion, which was to the east of the 3d, by dusk had forced its companies back more than 1,000 yards. With that, the 15th Infantry called a halt to operations for the day.

For the 3d Division, the day's fighting had yielded little more ground than on the 30th, but its regiments and battalions were ready to continue the struggle. Early on 1 February, General Truscott renewed the attack, with the 1st Battalion, 30th Infantry, moving out first. Able to make another 1,000 yards northeast along the Ponte Rotto–Cisterna road, the battalion reached the same ditch (although at a different section) used by the Rangers in their ill-fated maneuver. Here the Germans struck with a devastating artillery barrage and an infantry-armor counterattack, all before the Americans could dig in. This assault was stopped short by one man, Private Alton W. Knappenberger, who lived to get his Medal of Honor.

When the enemy struck, Knappenberger climbed to a knoll and, ignoring the enemy fire, destroyed with his automatic rifle a nearby enemy machine gun nest and all its occupants. Two Germans got within 20 yards and lobbed potato mashers at him, but he killed them both from his exposed position with one burst from his BAR. Another machine gun opened up on the spunky private; he wiped out this one, too. A German 20-mm antiaircraft gun then began blasting directly at Knappenberger. Unfazed, he instantly returned the fire and wounded one of the gun's crew members. Faced with both tank and artillery fire, Knappenberger shot at any enemy soldier he could see until his ammunition was gone. Then he crawled forward, replenished his supply from a downed comrade and resumed his personal battle with the Germans. Finally, his ammunition once again gone, he returned to his company, some 300 yards to the rear. For over two hours, according to the official citation, "Knappenberger's intrepid action disrupted the enemy attack," but the 1st Battalion, 30th Infantry, was still unable to advance any farther.

Meanwhile, the 1st Battalion, 15th Regiment, renewed the attack on the Division's right flank toward the Cisterna–Littoria road, a move now deemed essential by Truscott before trying once again for Cisterna itself. This attack also failed, and by noon on the 31st it was becoming clear that the 3d Division, with its wide front and worn down after almost three days of fighting of the most difficult kind, would not be able to take Cisterna, especially since the Germans were still sending in fresh reinforcements.

During the afternoon of the 1st, Major Sinsal reported that his beleaguered infantrymen—only a few of them were left—would have to be withdrawn, because the Germans obviously considered this salient to be a serious threat to their defenses. No sooner were Sinsal's men replaced than a fresh battalion from the 26th Panzer Division struck with fury on the morning of 2 February. The panzers were beaten off, however, with the help of Allied tanks, tank destroyers and artillery. The Germans tried again in the afternoon, but were again thrown back. The 7th Infantry had been able to hold on to its tenuous position, and in the process had virtually destroyed a battalion of the 26th Panzers.

But in spite of the strong stance taken by the 7th Infantry, by the afternoon of the 1st the 3d Division attack had lost its momentum. The division had suffered heavy losses. It had almost reached Cisterna, and it had inflicted many casualties on the German defenders, in some cases nearly destroying entire units. By that night the Germans seemed to have a distinct numerical superiority at Anzio, a situation that brought forth the specter of a devastating, possibly disastrous counterattack against VI Corps. The Allies were not to be disappointed, for as soon as the Germans were sure the corps attack had been halted, General von Mackensen and his Fourteenth Army staff began to make plans for a major move to eliminate what Hitler called the "abscess" below Rome.

6. Counterattack

While the newspapers were trumpeting the progress of the new offensive at Anzio, General Lucas's superiors—from Churchill through Marshall, Alexander and Wilson to Clark—were becoming increasingly dissatisfied with the situation at the beachhead. At this point Churchill was "much troubled with several features of the Anzio operation." His basic questions concerned VI Corps's hesitation to take towns such as Cisterna and Campoleone earlier in the offensive. And he wondered about the employment of American paratroops as regular infantry. Why had they not been dropped inland, as first intended? On 8 February, in a message to General Wilson, the Supreme Commander in the Mediterranean, Churchill expressed his disappointment. Regarding the way Alexander and Clark had handled Lucas, Churchill said pointedly that "senior commanders should not 'urge,' but 'order.'" The message was supposed to be revealed to General Marshall.

General Clark, who had moved his advance command post to Anzio, much to the chagrin of General Lucas, was also unhappy. His diary of 30 January recalled his frustration concerning not only Anzio but the entire Italian campaign: "The southern front [along the Gustav Line] is like two boxers in the ring, both about to collapse. I have committed my last reserve and I am sure the Boche has done the same." Concerning Anzio specifically, Clark went on to write that he was disappointed that VI Corps had not advanced farther, that although it would have been wrong to take the Alban Hills, a "reconnaissance in force with tanks should have been more aggressive to capture Cisterna and Campoleone." By the 31st, Clark was well aware that things would get "sticky." Although both the 1st and 3d Divisions were exhausted and needed a break, he could spare no more replacements from the Cassino area. Because of the current circumstances at Anzio, Clark also realized to his regret that Lucas had "no choice but to order our forces to dig in all along the front in expectation of a counterattack." Glumly, he added, "For the first time since Salerno, part of the Fifth Army was going on the defensive behind hastily laid mine fields and barbed wire."

Clark also felt keenly the loss of the Rangers, as did Truscott. The Fifth Army commander on the 31st visited 3d Division headquarters, where he told Truscott that he believed the Rangers were not suited for the task they had been given. In his diary, Clark wrote, "This was a definite error in judgment, for the Rangers do not have the support weapons to overcome the resistance indicated . . ."

After the landing, Anzio is bombarded by the Germans (note smoke)

Truscott believed differently.

"I reminded him [General Clark]," Truscott later said, "that I had been responsible for organizing the original Ranger battalion and that Colonel Darby and I perhaps understood their capabilities better than other American officers. He said no more. However, General Clark feared unfavorable publicity, for he ordered an investigation to fix responsibility. That was wholly unnecessary for the responsibility was entirely my own, especially since both Colonel Darby and I considered the mission a proper one, which should have been well within the capabilities of these fine soldiers. That ended the matter. The remnant of the Ranger force was returned to the United States a few weeks later."

As for General Lucas, he believed he had done his best. Clark wrote on the 30th, "I have been harsh with Lucas today, much to my regret, but in an effort to energize him to greater effort." On 1 February, Alexander visited the beachhead. Because of this trip and the previous admonitions from Clark, Lucas felt it necessary to sum up the situation in his diary:

"I am afraid he [Alexander] is not pleased. My head will probably fall in the basket but I have done my best. There were just too many Germans here for me to lick and they could build up faster than I could. As I told Clark yesterday, I was sent on a desperate mission, one where the odds were greatly against success, and I went without saying anything because I was given an order and my opinion was not asked. The condition in which I find myself is much better than I ever anticipated or had any right to expect."

The Germans had indeed seemed to build up their forces much faster than the Allies and their intelligence staffs had predicted they could. Around 1 February the Germans appeared to have numerical superiority in the area; parts of many enemy divisions were reported as being encountered by the Allies. In reality, however, this supposed enemy strength was what Kesselring called "a higgledy-piggledy jumble—units of numerous divisions fighting confusedly side by side." What was happening was that, when an element of a particular enemy division was identified, Allied intelligence analysts were assuming that the unit was on hand in its entirety. This was standard intelligence practice at the time, although criticized by some. The overestimation of the Germans' strength was underpinned by the stiffness of their resistance, but in actuality there were only about 90,000 German troops present during the last of January and the first of February, against nearly 100,000 Allied.

As the attacks of the 1st and 3d Divisions faded out on 1 February, no one could know how close VI Corps had come to defeating the Germans. Instead of attacking, as they had planned, the latter had been forced to go on the defensive. The Germans had had to use every reserve unit available, and they suffered approximately the same number of casualties as the

Allies—5,500 men. According to the official history, "Kesselring and Mackensen desperately juggled their troop units and just managed to hold. . . . To the Germans, the defensive stand bordered on the miraculous."

On 2 February, Alexander and Clark ordered Lucas to assume the defense, to hold the front line with as few troops as possible, supplementing it with mines and wire and other defensive measures, and to establish reserves sufficient to stop any large counterattack the enemy might be planning. Lucas was disappointed with the order. He did not believe that he should stop his offensive. "We must keep him [the enemy] off balance all we can," he wrote in his diary. So it was that the initiative passed to the Germans, and in time VI Corps would be taxed to the utmost just to preserve what little ground it had taken.

Just before the Germans counterattacked for the first time, they reorganized to some extent in the Anzio area to eliminate as much as they could of the "higgledy-piggledy" described by Kesselring. I Parachute Corps, which had been in command of the whole front under Fourteenth Army, was given the enemy right sector—west of the Albano Road extending to the Molleta River. I Corps had two divisions, 4th Parachute to the west and 65th Infantry to the east. To take care of the central and eastern sectors of the Allied perimeter, the staff of LXXVI Panzer Corps was transferred from the Tenth Army, where it had been opposing the British Eighth Army in the Adriatic area. From the Albano road eastward it had five divisions: 3d Panzer Grenadier, 715th Infantry (Motorized), 71st Infantry, Hermann Göring and 26th Panzer. Once again, a specially tailored combat group, still called Combat Group Graeser, was to lead the German attack. Mackensen planned to do three things: eliminate the Campoleone salient and retake the Factory, drive to the sea along the Albano road and then attack the Allied defenses along the Mussolini Canal.

On the night of 3 February the Germans began their first counterattack, a two-pronged effort to pinch out the Campoleone salient—occupied solely by the British 1st Division—from both the east and the west. It was a long front for one division to hold. Just before midnight the 1st Irish and 1st Scots Guards on the west side of the Albano road reported strong attacks; the same pressure was being felt soon on the east side of the salient. The Germans, by constricting the British in the middle, were trying to envelop the whole 3d Brigade.

As dawn broke it appeared that the western attack was the stronger; parts of the 65th Infantry Division actually penetrated the Irish Guard defenses. But it soon became clear that the more serious of the two threats was on the east, where the 6th Gordon Highlanders Battalion was making a stand. Under a cold, drizzling rain the German tanks penetrated deeply and their infantrymen came pouring in afterward. Because of the heavy cloud cover, there was little Allied air support, and by noon the danger of the 3d Brigade's being isolated loomed heavily. General Penney called on a battal-

The Factory

ion of the 168th Infantry Brigade, British 56th Division, which was being sent from the Garigliano River area, for a counterattack. This move helped stem the German advance, and as the day wore on the enemy attacks weakened. By nightfall the British were able to restore most of their lines. Casualties on both sides had been extremely heavy—the British had 1,400 killed, wounded or missing—because the fighting was not only fierce but close. That evening, however, General Lucas decided that the salient was too thinly held and the troops manning it were dangerously exposed. Before midnight the 1st Division withdrew to a line about a mile north of Carroceto and the Factory, and the 168th Infantry Brigade replaced the 3d Brigade in the center of the British sector. Although the Germans had not been able to encircle the 3d Brigade, they had realized their first objective, the elimination of the Campoleone salient.

While the fighting was in progress at Campoleone, General Lucas issued formal instructions confirming oral orders given on 3 February. These instructions concerned the way the VI Corps defenses were to be set up. Based on a "final beachhead line," the reorganization that was required to underpin the physical defense measures was extensive. Lucas considered the two flanks of the beachhead to be easily defensible. A regimental combat team from the 45th Division, which had completed its arrival in the area a few days earlier, was given responsibility for the Moletta River flank, and the 1st Special Service Force, also newly arrived, took care of the Mussolini Canal on the corps west flank. The center of the perimeter, at this point actually several miles north of the final line, was the responsibility of the 1st and 3d Divisions. The 1st Division—reinforced with additional tanks, tank destroyers, artillery and a battalion of the 504th Parachute Infantry Regiment—was to prepare a defense in depth from west of the Albano Road to Carano. The 3d Division—reinforced with tanks, tank destroyers, field artillery, automatic antiaircraft weapons, the 84th Chemical Battalion, the rest of the 504th, all of the 509th Parachute Infantry Battalion and what was left of the Rangers—was made responsible for the sector east of Carano to the point where the West Branch joined the Mussolini Canal. The 1st Armored Division, still minus Combat Command B, and the bulk of the 45th Infantry Division were held in corps reserve. General Harmon's 1st Armored was positioned east of the Albano road in the Padiglione Woods, while the two remaining regiments of the 45th Division, commanded by General Eagles, were situated just northeast of Nettuno along the road to Cisterna. Both the 1st Armored and the 45th Divisions were to organize strong defenses behind the final line in their respective areas. Also designated as corps reserve were two engineer regiments. Because their primary mission was engineering at the port, as well as port defense, they were required to be able to assemble and move within four hours' notice.

The preparation of the defense system was a demanding job, requiring great effort under the most trying conditions. During a front-line inspection on 6 February, General Clark approved the thoroughness with which the defenses had been set up, and he told Lucas to be ready to resume the offensive as soon as German pressure slackened. Almost everything that had been done to construct the fortifications and mutually supporting strongpoints was accomplished during dark, often during the tumult of battle. Although at first the system was rudimentary, it became stronger and more sophisticated as time went on. According to the official history:

German shell narrowly misses a DUKW off Anzio

"During the month of February, although powerful enemy attacks tore deep rents in the forward lines of defense, necessitating frequent shifts in the positions of the defending troops, the general outline of the VI Corps plan of defense remained intact."

After the action in the 1st Division sector at Campoleone, the Germans did not attack in strength for another three days. They did, however, shell the beachhead with regularity, and the Luftwaffe struck whatever targets it could. During this period General Clark bolstered a weak spot between the 1st and 3d Divisions with two more battalions from a 45th Division regiment. At the same time extra efforts were made to expedite the flow of replacements to the now depleted front-line divisions.

On 5 February the Germans made a strong probe against the 3d Infantry Division. After an intense concentration of artillery, tank and mortar fire, the Germans attacked with tanks and infantry against a thinly held part of the front just west of Ponte Rotto. According to General Truscott, the activity had "all the earmarks of the full-scale attack we were expecting and we watched developments tensely." Communication was established with the battalion commander, who, painting a picture of imminent disaster, requested permission from Truscott to withdraw. Not being able to think of any other course of action at the time, the 3d Division commander gave his permission, only to find out that this move caused the withdrawal of another battalion, to ensure that no flanks were exposed. As the result, Truscott found himself actually withdrawing along part of his front almost to the final beachhead line. Further developments proved that the attack was actually just an enemy probe, and Truscott quickly ordered his commanders to get back to the original lines at once. Little damage had been done, but fundamental weaknesses in the defenses had been revealed. Specifically, the commanders realized that preoccupation with preparation of the defense line had left the front lines too weak and had instilled in the GIs the thought that they did not have to hold at the front because of the strength to the rear. According to General Truscott, the commanders set about correcting this attitude at once.

Allied intelligence sources in Rome predicted that the next German attack would begin in the predawn hours of 7 February against the 3d Division. The 7th came and went in relative quietness, however, except for one tragic incident. A single German bomber being chased over the beachhead by a Spitfire unloaded its bombs to gain speed and altitude. The explosives fell in the middle of an area occupied by an evacuation hospital, killing and wounding nearly 100 people. Three Army nurses were among the dead. In a remarkable twist of fate the Luftwaffe pilot was shot down and given over to the same hospital, where he was treated. Because of the crowded conditions on the beach itself, this incident was not altogether avoidable. The Germans were usually careful not to hit hospitals, but by chance, as in the bombing incident, such facilities were often struck

Signal battalion soldiers repair communications in Nettuno

by artillery. The Allies, although having an ample supply of artillery ammunition (which would eventually perhaps spell the difference between winning or losing), were actually outgunned by the German heavy weapons. The enemy shelled the beachhead with regularity.

The reports from Rome were only partially correct. The German attack did begin on the 7th, but not until evening, and it was against the British 1st Division. The night was extremely dark, and the Germans took advantage of the darkness and of the extremely broken terrain to thrust deeply with their main attack into the British left-flank lines. Hand-to-hand fighting was commonplace, as infantry from the 65th Division came down the Buonriposo Ridge, hammering against positions of the British 24th Guards Brigade. Front-line strongpoints were soon overrun, and forward elements made their way back to alternate positions in the rear.

Although the British exhibited many acts of heroism that night, one stood out above the rest. Major W. P. Sidney, commander of a support company that was covering the withdrawal of the 5th Grenadier Guards, rallied his men to the defense. Covering Carroceto Creek with fire, this small band held off hundreds of Germans as they tried again and again to reach Carroceto and the Factory, and in effect their stand blunted the enemy onslaught. The 65th Division, however, had gained another objective, the Buonriposo Ridge, and proceeded to consolidate its positions.

Combat Group Graeser attacked the British right flank only a little later than the 65th Division assaulted on the left. This group used the same tactic—rapid infiltration—that was being used by the 65th Division against the other side of the British lines, and soon there were many small penetrations deep in the Allied defenses. But the 29th Panzer Grenadier Regiment, which spearheaded the attack, did not meet with success; British defenders were able to hold it to unimportant gains. One small group reached the rear of the Factory only to be gunned down by a lieutenant and his tank destroyer with its .50-caliber machine gun. In another part of the sector, the Germans were able to keep pressure on the 168th Brigade but were unable to capture a key lateral road just to the east of the Factory.

General Penney was mostly concerned about the precarious situation on his left. He moved the battalion of the 504th Parachute Regiment south of Carroceto to act as a counterattack force, and committed his reserve, the 3d Brigade—which had fought so hard to keep the Campoleone salient—ordering it to retake the Buonriposo Ridge. Two battalions of the 3d Brigade and a company of the 504th counterattacked, regained some ground and bolstered the beleaguered front-line infantry. Although the 1st Division had been seriously battered all day, and had taken heavy casualties, General Penney's men had checked the initial German assault.

In the 3d Division area, things were much quieter. Before dawn on the 8th one enemy tank column tried to make its way down the road from Cisterna to Isola Bella, only to be turned back by a company of the 15th Infantry. During the daylight hours there was just one attack—a raid against Carano—which was repulsed by the 509th Parachute Infantry. On the corps right flank, Brigadier General Robert T. Frederick's 1st Special Service Force, in a continuing pattern of stabbing at the enemy with hard-hitting patrols, staged a raid on Sessano. Special Service troops withdrew after holding the village for three hours, during which time they virtually destroyed the German company that held it.

In response to the German attacks, corps artillery began a coordinated, methodical effort to shell German positions across from the British lines. And an emergency request for help brought forth two British cruisers and one American, which increased greatly the number of five- and six-inch guns available to the offshore armada. Allied aircraft added more than usual to the bombardment because good weather made accurate observation possible. Dive-bombers were able to provide close air support, and medium bombers were active deeper in the enemy rear.

In spite of the more effective than usual air, artillery and naval gunfire

support, which took its toll among Mackensen's ground forces, the Fourteenth Army renewed its attack with fervor on the 9th. Mortar and artillery
fire preceded use of the tactic employed the day before—infiltration of
British lines at night. On the British left flank the German 65th Infantry
Division, in a supporting attack, forced the 5th Grenadier Guards back to
the Carroceto station and to the old railway-bed overpass over the Albano
road. The 3d Brigade and Parachute Infantry elements which, the afternoon before, had regained parts of the Buonriposo Ridge were also thrown
back, this time to a stream south of that high ground. Combat Group
Graeser was responsible for the main effort for the day against the British
right flank, and General Graeser now felt obliged to use his last reserve to
ensure success. Four regiments were thus to be thrown against the British
168th Brigade and the Factory. After infiltrating small units during dark,
the Germans struck with force at daylight, and fighting soon spread across
the entire front of the 168th. East of the Factory at one locaion the enemy
gained over a mile, and at another spot they overran a company-held
strongpoint. Exploiting the situation rapidly, the Germans brought up
tanks and self-propelled guns, and just before noon they took the Factory.

The British left flank protecting Carroceto was still mostly intact as
General Harmon entered the fray with two companies of the 1st Armored

U.S. self-propelled 105-mm howitzers fire on enemy positions

Division. Counterattacking the hard-pressing Germans, light tanks moved against the Buonriposo Ridge. Company A thwarted one enemy surge, but Company B met the fate that was usual in the area. Its tanks became mired in the mud after leaving the road, and seven were lost as a result of the intense fire that followed. Around noon two more tank companies were sent to help, this time in the vicinity of the Factory. Both companies enjoyed limited success, but Aprilia by now was bristling with antitank guns. One of the tank companies was able to give the British some help in mopping up German penetrations east of the Factory, but that was about all before fighting slackened late in the afternoon.

The coordinated Allied air, artillery and naval bombardment that had started on the 8th was continued on the 9th, but with less success because a strong gale held down the air observation necessary for close air support. One of the offshore British destroyers was slightly damaged by German artillery fire and forced to retire for repairs. Fifth Army did request as much air support as possible, and a resulting bombardment of German assembly areas near Campoleone proved effective.

By dusk the fighting had subsided. Both sides had suffered heavy casualties and were nearly exhausted, and as a result reorganization and consolidation was the rule during the night. Although three brigades of the 1st Division were on the front line, two of them protecting Carroceto, overall division strength was only about 50 percent of that authorized. There was no question in the minds of the Anzio generals, including Lucas, that another division was needed to hold the beachhead until an Allied breakout could occur along the Gustav Line.

Since the Germans now held the Factory, they used its tall buildings to an advantage. Late on 9 January they began to shell British positions around Carroceto, the buildings serving as observation points. After midnight on the 10th German tanks moved out in force from the Factory, heading for Carroceto. This first attack was broken up, but at 0430 the enemy renewed the effort, and for the British north of Carroceto the situation became grave. All contact had been lost with two forward companies, while other units were forced to withdraw to the overpass still held by the battered 5th Grenadier Guards. At 0530 General Penney reported to VI Corps that without relief he could not hold on. As a result, Allied air and artillery support was concentrated on the Germans as close to the British lines as possible, but by mid-morning increasingly heavier cloud cover precluded further tactical air assistance. The British lost Carroceto station during the morning, retook it in the afternoon and lost it again in the evening. The fighting was continuously heavy, but massing and concentration of Allied air and artillery support—especially the artillery—had taken a heavy toll in the German ranks. Although Fourteenth Army had taken its initial objectives, the three days of fighting were costly. The Germans were too exhausted to press the advance.

Major General
William W. Eagles

General Lucas then ordered two regiments of the 45th Division to relieve the depleted and worn-out 1st Division of a considerable portion of its front line. Since Lucas deemed the recapture of the Factory essential, the 45th Division commander, General Eagles, planned an immediate counterattack to get it. On 11 February, after a 15-minute artillery concentration, a plan to strike Aprilia through the overpass and also from the southeast was put into play. Attached tank companies led each of the infantry attacks, but both had been stopped by strong opposition by noon. At 1300 the Americans pressed on again. This time both leading tank companies reached the Factory, and the close fighting that followed raged on for the entire afternoon. Tanks on either side were destroyed, and the confusion of battle was intense both in the town and at its outskirts. But as the day waned the Americans were forced once again to withdraw. General Eagles ordered his men to try again on the 12th, only to have them thrown back once more, in spite of one of the heaviest air bombardments of the campaign. Late on the 12th, both the Allies and the Germans in effect called a halt to operations. Each was in dire need of rest, resupply and reorganization. But the Allies had held on.

93

7. Action at Cassino

During the last few days of January, and on in to February, things were not much better on the southern front than they were at Anzio. The Allied lineup had not changed a great deal during the period. General Leese's Eighth Army, responsible for the front from Fifth Army's right flank to the Adriatic Sea, still had the quieter of the two sectors. In the Fifth Army zone, General Juin's French Expeditionary Corps was facing the Germans along the northern section of the Gustav Line. South of the French was the II Corps of Major General Geoffrey Keyes, whose battered 36th Division had just been repulsed in a bloody attempt to cross the Rapido River. From the II Corps left flank to the Tyrrhenian Sea the British X Corps, with Lieutenant General Sir Richard McCreery in command, had successfully crossed the lower Garigliano River and was holding fast to what little ground had been gained.

By the time the last of the 36th Division infantrymen had returned under fire to the east bank of the Rapido on 22 January, Operation Shingle was off to a good start. Field Marshal Kesselring had already made the decision to reinforce as quickly as possible in the Anzio area, and General Vietinghoff's Tenth Army, holding the Gustav Line, felt the pinch immediately. Early in the morning of the 22d, the Tenth Army commander was or-

94

dered to transfer to Anzio a corps headquarters and all the troops he could spare. Before the day was out, the newly arrived I Parachute Corps, the 3d Panzer Grenadier Division (less one regiment), the 71st Division and parts of the Hermann Göring Division—all facing the Fifth Army—had begun to leave for Anzio.

Although the transfer of German troops to Anzio had weakened the enemy defenses across from McCreery's corps, the general could not take advantage of this development. His soldiers were in need of rest and resupply and were temporarily unable to continue the offensive. General Alphonse Juin's French corps was in the process of shifting troops to the southern portion of its sector, in preparation for an attack on Monte Belvedere, about five miles north of Cassino, on 25 January. II Corps, in the middle, was selected to carry on the job of trying to get through the still formidable German defenses. Since the 36th Division was in no condition to make another attempt at a river crossing south of Highway 6, General Clark directed an attack against Cassino, to be conducted by the American 34th Infantry Division, commanded by Major General Charles W. Ryder. General Keyes ordered Ryder to cross the Rapido where it could be forded, then break into a two-pronged drive to take Cassino and to penetrate the Cassino massif, an area that took in the mountains to the west of

General Heinrich von Vietinghoff

GIs fire a bazooka in the Rapido area

Cassino and included the soon-to-be-famous Monte Cassino and its abbey. After penetrating the massif, the 34th Division was to enter the Liri Valley behind Monte Cassino. Ryder began his attack at 2200 on the 24th, and succeeded the first day in getting three battalions of the 133d Infantry Regiment across the river. The Germans were determined to hold the line, however, and the American infantry on the 25th could do little more than cross the river and consolidate their tenuous hold on the west bank. German fire coming from the high ground to the west was devastating and unrelenting, but even though the 133d could not advance over the next 24 hours, it still held on.

During the night of the 26th Ryder sent part of the 135th Regiment across the river just south of the 133d's toehold, in the hope of seizing the heights from which the Germans were keeping the GIs pinned down in the bridgehead. On the 27th, prodded by Keyes, Ryder decided to send in two battalions of his third regiment, the 168th, directing them to pass through the 133d, preceded by tanks. Several tanks actually got across but were soon destroyed. But several companies followed and were able to hold fast. At one point the opposition was stiff enough to convince one company commander that he had to withdraw. This action precipitated a self-induced rout to the rear by several companies. Finally stopped at the west bank by their leaders, these units were withdrawn across the river. They were reorganized, and then back they came across the Rapido about 500 yards to the north. There they dug in. Now they were able to protect a potential tank crossing site.

While Ryder's division was making small but hard-fought inroads near Cassino, the French Expeditionary Corps jumped off on its planned attack. Monte Belvedere was an important Fifth Army objective, a hill whose

96

capture represented a real threat to the Germans. After two days of intense fighting, Major General Aimé de Goislard de Monsabert's 3d Algerian Division took the mountain's heights. Monsabert's soldiers needed a rest, however, before they could try for Monte Abate. Fifth Army wanted Abate in order to protect the 34th Division's right flank should it be successful in penetrating the Cassino massif, but General Juin informed headquarters that he needed help. He had no corps reserves, and his divisions were spread too thin on a very long front. If the 34th Division was unable to move farther west, Juin added, he would be forced to abandon Monte Belvedere. The 3d Algerian Division was simply too isolated with its highly vulnerable flanks.

General Clark had already sensed the weakness, however, and told General Keyes to put another unit between the 34th Division and the 3d Algerian. Retaining General Harmon's Combat Command B for an exploiting thrust, Keyes chose the 142d Infantry Regiment, 36th Division, for the job. Meanwhile, as the 142d was en route to the Monte Belvedere area, Ryder committed the remaining battalion of the 168th Regiment, giving it the task of taking high ground that would make possible a thrust to Monte Castellone.

Because the Allied actions north of Highway 6 seemed to be eroding the German defenses and thus offering a chance to penetrate the Gustav Line, all the Allied leaders moved quickly. On the 29th, with extra engineer and tank support, preceded by an intense artillery preparation, the 168th, now using all three of its battalions, attacked again. The going was hard, but many tanks got across the Rapido. By dawn the next day both the tanks and the three battalions occupied the hills west of Cairo. Likewise on the 29th, the 142d Regiment made its move between the American 34th and 3d Algerian Divisions. This effort turned into a two-day attack between Monte Castellone and Monte Belvedere.

Although the village of Cairo was captured by the 168th Infantry on the 30th, that day and the next proved difficult for the rest of the regiment, which occupied the hills west of the village. Communication between the various positions was just about nonexistent, because the radios had become wet during the river crossing. But three German counterattacks were nevertheless beaten off. Even so, all the tanks that had made it across the river could go no farther than the base of the steep hills. Under intense German fire, directed by well-placed observers and coming from well-implaced artillery and mortar positions, the tanks simply huddled against the base of the precipitous heights and watched while several light tanks bringing up supplies were picked off by the Germans.

In reality, none of the Fifth Army's three corps on the southern front made much important headway. Even General McCreery's X Corps, during an offensive thrust to the west on 27 January, expanded its holdings only slightly. Although the 34th Division's newly won bridgehead near

Cassino was a step in the right direction, the ground captured was not decisive terrain, and the capture of Monte Belvedere by the French corps represented only a bend, not a break, in the Gustav Line. It was at this time in the Italian campaign that General Clark likened the situation to the two boxers in the ring, "both about to collapse."

The Germans, too, had had a difficult time, and the intense fighting along the Gustav Line brought forth reinforcements even though the battles at Anzio were beginning to reach a high pitch. Across from McCreery's X Corps was the German 94th Division and some of the 29th Panzer Grenadier Division. Facing II Corps were three divisions that had sent some of their battalions to Anzio—15th Panzer Grenadier, 71st Infantry and 3d Panzer Grenadier. The entire 44th Infantry Division was also in line along the sector. Opposing the French were parts of the 3d Panzer Grenadiers and all of the 5th Mountain Division. All the German units had been at the front for at least a month, and besides the intense fighting, the severe weather that was hindering the Allies likewise made things worse for Tenth Army. To help out in the critical Cassino area, General von Vietinghoff brought in from the Adriatic front the 90th Panzer Grenadier Division, followed by part of the highly respected 1st Parachute Division. Other units of this latter division had already been rushed to Anzio. These

Major General
Charles W. Ryder

98

moves now enabled all of the 29th Panzers to be sent to General von Mackensen's Fourteenth Army at Anzio. The elements of the 1st Parachute Division that had been sent to Anzio rejoined their comrades at Cassino during the second week in February, where once more they would prove their right to their reputation for bravery and doggedness.

General Alexander, too, decided to shift units between his two armies. The British Eighth Army had already been tapped twice for divisions—the 1st for Anzio and the 5th for II Corps—when Alexander transferred another division, the 2d New Zealand, to the Cassino area. Hence Lieutenant General Sir Oliver Leese, in order to continue his offensive plans, took the I Canadian Corps Headquarters and the 4th Indian Division from his reserves for action on his front. Then, on 30 January, Alexander called for the 4th Indian Division. General Leese, now short four entire divisions, was therefore compelled to drop any notions of an offensive. While waiting for a break in the Gustav Line, Alexander on 3 February established a temporary corps headquarters, the New Zealand Corps, under the New Zealand division commander, Lieutenant General Sir Bernard Freyberg, a famous and adventurous soldier in both world wars. Both the 2d and the 4th divisions would be under his command. The New Zealand Corps was then attached to Fifth Army to exploit any breakthrough that might be made in the Gustav Line.

General Ryder's two-pronged attack, which he had started late on 24 January, was still making headway, inch by inch, on 1 February. The 34th Division commander sent the 133d to take an Italian barracks—already the scene of hard fighting—near Cassino. This strongpoint was finally captured on the 2d. Meanwhile, the 135th Regiment passed through the 169th, which had been holding the hills west of Cairo, and made a thrust toward Monte Castellone. During this same time, the 36th Division's 142d Regiment continued its drive between II Corps and the Algerians on Monte Belvedere. Heavy fog shielded the ground troops from German eyes, and the 142d took Mass Manna while the 168th captured Monte Castellone. As the 34th Division's various regiments were consolidating their positions on 1 February, General Ryder sent an infantry and a tank battalion from the barracks to try to capture Cassino town itself, but this move was halted by machine gun and antitank fire some two miles from the village.

At this point, however, the Allies were heartened by the situation. Cassino—the key to the Liri Valley and the link-up with Anzio—at last seemed to be within reach. General Clark himself was optimistic. "The Cassino heights," he told Alexander, "will be captured very soon." In the same message, Clark asked Alexander's advice concerning the use of the New Zealand Division, and it was at this point that the *ad hoc* corps was formed. The New Zealanders and Indians were thus positioned, along with Harmon's Combat Command B of the U.S. 1st Armored Division, where they could exploit a breakthrough by the 34th Division into the Liri Valley.

Clark relieved the 36th Division, then still in position south of Highway 6, with the New Zealanders, and put the rest of the units in locations where they could easily move forward.

While these maneuvers were going on, the 34th Division was still making limited progress. Both this division and the 3d Algerian Division were beginning to make a noticeable swing to the south. The Algerians took over Mass Manna, while the 142d moved down to Monte Castellone. The 135th and the 133d did likewise, the latter moving along a mountainous shelf to Cassino where they succeeded in reaching the northern edge of town. The combat in the village was desperate street fighting at its deadliest, and because Cassino seemed so close the battle continued unabated until 4 February. Fighting for the massif around Cassino was no less difficult, and it too continued without respite. As the 4th drew to a close, General Ryder simply had to call a halt to the attempts to take the village. The 34th Division had joined the ranks of the seriously depleted and exhausted units of the Fifth Army. The men had to get some rest. For three days the division refitted, as General Ryder prepared for a supreme effort to take the town.

On the 8th, II Corps renewed the push. General Keyes moved the 36th Division to the right of the 34th to strengthen any south-swinging envelopment when Cassino and the dominating Monte Cassino were taken. Late on the 7th General McCreery's X Corps had made an attempt to thrust north to the Liri. General Juin was also asked to attack, making it a simultaneous three-corps advance, but the French were still too exhausted

Mark Clark wanted "the Cassino heights"

to participate. The II Corps drive was quickly stymied, and six days later the 133d was still hammering at Cassino. Fighting had been so vicious and so demoralizing to the Allies, especially the 34th Division, that Fifth Army called the offensive to a halt. The 36th Division was only about "25 percent of effective combat strength," it was reported, and one regiment in the 34th Division had an average of only 30 men in its rifle companies. II Corps had come within a mile of Highway 6, keeping alive the idea of a breakthrough. The New Zealand Corps with its two divisions would be the next to try.

The 4th Indian Division relieved Ryder's tired and depleted 34th, and General Freyberg scheduled an attack for February 14th. Freyberg, an imposing figure with a great deal of hard-won prestige, called for air support in the form of an attack against the ancient Benedictine abbey on Monte Cassino, which so far had remained virtually unscathed. Freyberg feared that the abbey was being used for artillery observation. He insisted that it had to be destroyed to ensure the success of his ground forces. Clark disagreed, but Alexander upheld Freyberg's request, and in one of the most argued and criticized Allied moves of the war, the abbey was bombed on 15 February. But the move did not help the Allied advance. It was learned later that, although the Germans had positions close to the abbey, they had not used the building itself. The principal military result of the bombing was to create a mass of ruins that provided the Germans with strong defensive positions. The southern front would remain in stalemate for weeks to come. No one would be moving north to Anzio.

Cassino castle (foreground) undergoes American bombardment

8. The Second 20 Days

During the first two weeks of February the atmosphere at the Anzio beachhead was anything but cheery. On the 12th the 45th Division had failed in its last attempt to retake the Factory, and General Lucas's officers and men were beginning to realize what it was like to be constantly on guard, on the defensive, instead of pushing out, as in the offense. It was hardly the kind of action favored by General Patton, who believed that "in war, the only sure defense is offense, and the efficiency of offense depends on the warlike souls of those conducting it." Instead, the confrontation had turned into a tenacious Allied stance similar to that of the American Colonel George Croghan, remembered for his reply to a British request for surrender in the War of 1812: "We give up the fort when there is not a man left to defend it." This was the attitude that prevailed at Anzio. For a few days, beginning on the 12th, there were no major battles at the front lines; most of the action resulted from contacts made as the result of active patrolling on both sides. The resoluteness of the VI Corps defense was soon to be tested, however, if the G-2 staff was correct. Prisoners of war, describing changes General von Mackensen was making in front of General Lucas's lines, also revealed when Fourteenth Army would make its maximum effort: 0630, 16 February.

Allied leaders, Churchill in particular, were far from pleased with the situation in Italy, especially at Anzio. In a message on 10 February to General Alexander, responding to a previous report he had received concerning vehicle and personnel strength at the beachhead, Churchill voiced his increasing concern: "How many of our men are driving or looking after eighteen thousand vehicles in this narrow space? We must have a great superiority of chauffeurs. I am shocked that the enemy have more infantry than we . . ."

In his history of World War II Churchill revealed his real concern over the lack of VI Corps aggressiveness at this point.

> "All this was a great disappointment at home and in the United States. I did not of course know what orders had been given to General Lucas, but it is a root principle to push out and join the issue with the enemy, and it would seem that his judgment was against it from the beginning. As I said at the time, I had hoped that we were hurling a wildcat into the shore, but all we got was a stranded whale. The spectacle of eighteen thousand vehicles accumulated ashore by the fourteenth day for only seventy thousand men, or less than four men to a vehicle, including drivers and attendants, though they did not move more than twelve or fourteen miles, was astonishing."

Churchill was amazed at how quickly the Germans were able to move their units and make adjustments in the "perilous gaps" on the southern front, and suggested to Alexander that he need not be concerned about "ordering" instead of "urging" the American commanders to advance. Alexander replied that he appreciated Churchill's advice and realized the disappointment the situation had caused, but that he had "every hope and intention of reaching the goal we set out to gain." This message was dated 11 February, four days before the Germans launched the most determined of all their counterattacks.

Generals Alexander and Clark were themselves growing increasingly dissatisfied with General Lucas's performance, a dissatisfaction no doubt reinforced by Churchill's voiced displeasure. Clark was, he later said, already considering a change in the command of VI Corps. General Lucas knew that his performance had not pleased his two superiors. On the 15th he observed, "I am afraid the top side is not completely satisfied with my work . . . They are naturally disappointed that I failed to chase the Hun out of Italy but there was no military reason why I should have been able to do so. In fact, there is no military reason for 'Shingle.' " General Wilson's deputy commander visited VI Corps headquarters on 16 February and repeated that higher levels thought that Lucas should have been more daring. Lucas was firm in his conviction, however, and wrote that had he pressed on to Rome he would have lost the corps, and that the prestige and

Ships continue to unload in Anzio harbor

morale of the enemy would have been raised. Anyway, he added, "my orders didn't read that way."

Mackensen felt obliged to make significant changes in the disposition of his Fourteenth Army troops before he was able to attack again. Having captured his initial objectives—the Campoleone salient and the Factory—he knew that he must continue to advance as quickly as possible. But the Fourteenth Army commander was not at all sure that he was strong enough to push the Allies into the sea. In any event, he did not attack until he had made all the preparations he deemed necessary, since it was unlikely that he would have another opportunity to do it.

Reinforcements had arrived for the Fourteenth Army, increasing its chances for success. From the Tenth Army came the veteran 29th Panzer Grenadier Division, from Yugoslavia came the 114th Division, and the 362d Division arrived from northern Italy. Mackensen was required, however, to return several 71st Division units to the Tenth Army front. To punctuate his concern for the relief of the situation at Anzio, Hitler sent the Berlin-Spandau Infantry Lehr Regiment, a special unit used to demonstrate to the German infantry just how an attack was supposed to be made. But much to the chagrin of both Kesselring and Mackensen, Hitler ordered that the Lehr Regiment make the initial attack, although it had no combat experience. Hitler also ordered Kesselring to have Mackensen attack on a narrow front in conjunction with a creeping barrage, a standard World War I tactic well remembered by Hitler. Although the two German commanders did not feel they could take issue with the orders to make a narrow frontal attack and to use the Lehr Regiment, even though they regarded them as tactically unsound, they did not employ the barrage strategy because of a shortage of ammunition.

104

On 9 February, Mackensen issued his orders for the German counterattack. West of the Albano road the assault was to be controlled by the I Parachute Corps; east of the road the LXXVI Corps was in command. Six divisions were to comprise the first attack wave: 3d Panzer Grenadier, 114th Light Infantry, 715th Infantry and parts of the Hermann Göring Division, under LXXVI Corps; and parts of the 4th Parachute and all of the 65th Infantry, under I Corps. Two divisions, the 26th and 29th Panzer Grenadiers, and two battalions of Tiger tanks were held in reserve to follow up after the first assault had punctured the Allied lines. As far as personnel were concerned, Fourteenth Army had an estimated 120,000 men in its ranks, 70,000 of whom were combat troops, while VI Corps fielded around 100,000 men.

The enemy plan was basic—simply to break Lucas's lines by massed infantry attacks backed up with tanks, then quickly follow with the reserves. During the main attack, Mackensen planned to hold the rest of the perimeter with as few troops as possible. A diversion in the form of merely assembling the reserve armored units in front of the 3d Division was also to be attempted. Although Mackensen himself was not sure that he would be able to succeed, the German high command had no doubts. Had not the Führer personally approved the Fourteenth Army's plan? The Germans hoped to win because of sheer superiority of men and some kinds of equipment, but they knew better than to underestimate the tenacity of Lucas's infantrymen and tankers. They knew, too, that VI Corps had more than an adequate supply of artillery ammunition and that naval gunfire could always be called on for assistance. The Germans were also well aware that the Allies enjoyed air superiority.

Although the VI Corps had been engaged in battle for some time without respite, spirits were good, and reinforcements sent in by General Clark enhanced both morale and the capability for putting up a lengthy defense. Clark sent the first of the 56th Division's brigades—the 168th, on 3 February—to help the 1st Division hold on to the Campoleone salient. The remaining two brigades, the 167th and the 169th, arrived at Anzio on 13 and 18 February. With the arrival of the 167th, the 1st Division reverted to VI Corps reserve.

On the eve of the German attack, front-line responsibilities were somewhat reorganized. The 3d Division still held the right half of the defensive line, but almost everything else was changed. The left flank along the Moletta River was now held by the 36th Engineers. From the Moletta to a point just west of the Albano Road, the front was secured by the two brigades of the 56th Division. The center portion of the defense was held by the 45th Division with all three of its regiments; from left to right were the 157th, the 179th and the 180th Infantry. Thus it was that across the most likely German avenue of approach General Lucas had placed relatively fresh infantry units. Artillery reinforcements were also received at

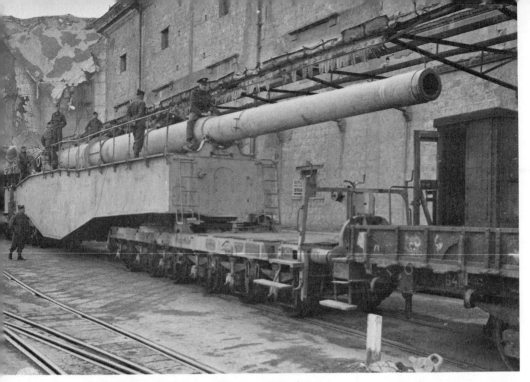

"Anzio Annie"—German 280-mm railroad gun

the beachhead, and with the plentiful supply of 105- and 155-mm howitzer ammunition the Allies enjoyed a distinct light and medium artillery advantage. According to the official history, by 14 February VI Corps guns were firing "about 20,000 rounds per day, and Allied destroyers and cruisers thickened the artillery fire almost daily." This contrasted with the enemy's average daily fire rate of about 1,500 rounds.

The MAAF tried to ward off, or at least minimize, the German attack by flying continuous bombing missions around Anzio. As of the 15th, some 26,000 sorties had been chalked up. One of the air priorities was the destruction of as many of the Germans' heavy guns as possible, a difficult task at best. The potent railroad guns, especially, were hard to target because they could move about with relative ease. These huge 280-mm cannon could be destroyed, however. On 14 February the two monsters were attacked by P-40s and shelled by VI Corps artillery whose fire was adjusted by P-51 observers. One gun was shattered and the other derailed in one of the more successful attacks against the heavy artillery.

On the afternoon of the 15th the Germans increased the tempo of their artillery fire against the beachhead forces, and the Luftwaffe became more than usually active. The entire beachhead came under attack, forcing the defenders to seek cover. An LCT loaded with gasoline was destroyed, and a Liberty ship was damaged. The official history describes this artillery and air attack in vivid terms.

"Heavy-caliber shells whistled over the front lines toward the harbor, where they threw up geysers of water or crashed into buildings, continuing the work of destroying the summer hotels and palatial villas along the water's edge. Defending antiaircraft guns filled the sky with high altitude 90-mm. shells and with a criss-cross pattern of 40-mm. red tracer shells which shot up like balls of light from dozens of Roman candles."

That night it was relatively quiet, with only a few artillery rounds coming in and with little activity at the front. In the predawn darkness, the quiet was almost foreboding.

The Germans attacked just as planned, one day after the bombing of the abbey on Monte Cassino. At precisely 0600 Mackensen's guns opened up along the center of the Allied front lines with an artillery preparation that lasted a half an hour. Then waves of gray-green assault troops hit the 45th Division's six-mile-long sector. Enemy soldiers from two divisions, the 3d Panzer Grenadier and the 715th Infantry, struck the left and center of the 45th Division, held by the 157th and 159th Infantry. The Factory and Carroceto provided observation posts enabling the Germans to watch all of the 179th's defensive sector and to pour observed fire almost directly into the Allied positions. When enemy tanks and infantry became low on ammunition, they simply pulled back to the Factory for more. All during the morning, the 179th thwarted attack after attack. According to an official account, "The enemy seemed to pay no attention to casualties. As fast as one wave of the attackers was broken it was replaced by another."

A 179th Regiment forward observer who had his OP in a farmhouse southeast of the Factory refused to withdraw when his position was attacked by both tanks and infantry. Finally struck in the head by a machine pistol round, he was left for dead, only to be captured alive by the Ger-

U.S. engineers plant antitank mines

mans. But he was recaptured minutes later, when the artillery fire he had been directing forced his captors to withdraw. Late in the afternoon, after yielding only a little insignificant ground, the 179th was given a chance to regroup when the enemy slowed the attack. The American infantry had taken heavy losses. One company reported as it gathered the remnants of its personnel that it was down to 30 men and had lost all its machine guns.

The Germans took heavy losses, too. The supposedly crack Infantry Lehr Regiment, which had been in on the attack against the 179th, broke under the strain of the resistance and fell back in disorder and without permission. Meanwhile, Allied artillery took a heavy toll among the rest of the attackers, both infantry and armored units. As an example, artillery that morning knocked out at least seven German tanks, its fires having been observed and placed accurately by Sergeant Charles W. Keyser, another tanker. Leading the remains of his unit—two tanks—Keyser then went on to destroy or damage several of those of the enemy as well as to fend off an infantry attack. The radio in his own tank was out of commission, and, having failed to hear his company commander order him to withdraw, Keyser spotted six more German tanks coming at him. He tried to make a run for it, laying down his own smoke screen, but his tank was hit and the driver killed. Keyser managed to make it back to his battalion after dark, badly burned. Altogether, he had been responsible for putting out of commission at least 10 German tanks.

The 157th Regiment, generally astride the Albano road to the left of the 179th, was hit by the Germans with almost as much force. After the initial artillery barrage, German tanks and infantry struck at Companies E and G of the 2d Battalion (the Battle of the Caves), which were holding the extreme left of the 45th Division sector and were in contact with the British. E Company held out against wave after wave of attackers, although one of its platoons was overrun. Allied artillery took care of the tanks attacking G Company, and the men in the foxholes took care of the accompanying German soldiers. Although its 3d Platoon was nearly eliminated, the rest of G Company held out all day against attack after attack and repeated attempts by the Germans to infiltrate its lines. Late in the afternoon, tanks actually penetrated the company's perimeter, but they were soon destroyed. The enemy failed to follow up, and the fighting in this part of the front—the critical Albano road area—died away for the day. The Germans had meanwhile made no inroads against the 45th Division's right flank, held by the 180th Infantry.

Attacks against the 56th and 3d Divisions and the 509th Parachute Infantry Battalion were not as strong as those against the 45th, since they were generally intended to be diversionary. Combat Group Berger, committing two waves of infantry and tanks against the 3d Division's 7th and 30th Regiments, penetrated about 300 yards before being repulsed with extremely heavy losses. Smaller probes against the 509th were thwarted with

Tank destroyer employs natural camouflage

little difficulty, but against the 56th Division the enemy was somewhat more successful. Crossing the Moletta River and driving down the Buonriposo Ridge, the Germans reached the final beachhead line before they were stopped.

They did not wait long to resume the offensive against the 45th Division. Just before midnight they again went on the attack along the Albano road. Company E of the 179th took the brunt of what was at first an infiltration tactic, and by dawn, with a few tanks and only 18 infantrymen left, it found itself surrounded, battling wave after wave of Germans and fighting for sheer survival. Knocking out enemy tanks, and then using smoke, the remnants of the force fought their way out of the trap, but a dangerous gap had been opened between the 179th and the 157th. The Germans exploited this success quickly, and aided by Luftwaffe fighters—Focke-Wulf 190s and Messerschmitt 109s—hit two battalions of the 179th head on.

By 0900 these units had been forced back almost to the final line. Time after time the infantry came at them, supported by dozens of tanks operating in small groups. One American company had been virtually destroyed, and to assist the struggling 45th Division all the artillery and air support available to VI Corps—truly a powerful force—was brought to bear

109

Gls dug in along the Mussolini Canal

in direct support of the front-line soldiers. Naval guns, 432 pieces of corps
and division artillery, 90-mm antiaircraft guns in direct fire, and aircraft
from fighters to B-24s and B-17s unleashed their shells and bombs, often
only a few hundred yards to the front of the infantry. According to the official history, the total number of bombers used and weight of bombs
dropped was truly enormous—the "greatest up to that date ever allotted in
direct support of an army." During the afternoon the Germans threw in
more fresh battalions against the beleaguered 179th, bringing the total to
14. They pushed as far south as the first Albano road overpass above Anzio,
just short of the final beachhead line, striving to deepen their newly won
salient.

Late in the morning General Harmon counterattacked with his tanks,
helping to hold the enemy north of the overpass but not regaining any lost
ground. To add more depth to the defense, General Lucas then ordered
the 1st Division, less one brigade, to hold the two miles of the beachhead
line to the east and west of Albano road. He also strengthened the Allied
units on the shoulders of the German salient. In an effort to regain some of
the lost ground, General Eagles sent his two depleted and weary regiments—the 157th and the 159th—forward in a counterattack after dark.
Under intense fire and incessant enemy pressure this attack also failed. As
dawn came on the 18th, so did the real crisis.

Actually two crises were developing on 17 February, the one on the
battlefield and a personal one for General Lucas. General Clark, in a move
that presaged a change in command of VI Corps, named General Truscott
as the deputy commander of the corps. Although Lucas had not yet lost his
job, he knew what was coming. In his diary he penned these thoughts:

"I think this means my relief. I hope that I am not to be relieved of command. I knew when I came in here that I was jeopardizing my career because I knew the Germans would not fold up because of two divisions landing on their flank. . . . I do not feel that I should have sacrificed my command [by taking the Alban Hills]."

Other command changes occurred that same day, although not of the same magnitude or meaning. General Penny, wounded by a shell fragment, was replaced by Major General G. W. R. Templer, who was to command both the 56th and the 1st Divisions. Taking General Truscott's place in the 3d Division was the colorful Brigadier General John W. ("Iron Mike") O'Daniel; and Colonel Darby, transferred after some delay to the 45th Division, took over command of the 179th Regiment. But on the night of the 17th General Lucas had far more important things on his mind. The crisis on the field of battle was getting worse by the minute.

Although General Eagles's counterattack early on the 18th made little progress, VI Corps hoped that it would at least disrupt German preparations for renewal of their own effort. Lucas and Truscott were encouraged that no further penetrations had been made by the enemy, even though they were not exactly sure what was going on because of the difficulty the divisions were having contacting their units. But the generals were deeply concerned at the fact that the four-mile-deep salient contained parts of at least six German divisions. On the morning of the 18th General Clark joined Lucas and Truscott at the VI Corps command post, an old wine cellar. A counterattack was decided on as the best way to deal with the worsening crisis. It would be a simple converging movement against the enemy salient from two different directions with two "forces." Force H, under General Harmon, with the 30th Infantry (3d Division) and his own 6th Armored Infantry, was to attack northwest out of the Padiglione Woods to the right of the Albano road along an open area and road known as the "Bowling Alley." Force T, under General Templer, consisted only of the

Major General
Ernest N. Harmon

169th Brigade, which was in the process of arriving in the Anzio area. Templer was to attack north from the overpass. Actual plans for the counterattack were completed around noon on the 18th, and the two commanders began immediately to prepare for its execution on the 19th.

Meanwhile, the enemy began what was his supreme effort to crack Lucas's final beachhead line. The first thrust occurred at dawn, and went deep into the positions of the still-intact but considerably depleted 179th Regiment. One 3d Battalion company was soon destroyed in detail, however, and only remnants of the battalion were able to filter back to the final defensive line, as German tanks and infantry were pushing south in increasing numbers.

Company I, 3d Battalion of the 157th Infantry, holding fast directly in front of the overpass, was in its second day of such attacks. According to the official history,

> "the ring of barbed wire surrounding the company was littered with bodies of dead and moaning Germans who only a few moments before had been shouting confidently, 'At ease, Company I. Watch out, Company I, here we come!' "

That company took a pounding. Five of the company officers were killed, wounded had to be left in waterlogged trenches, men remaining had had no food for two days, no sleep could be had in the cold of the night and German artillery was incessant. In spite of all this, the men of Company I repulsed everything the Germans could muster in the attack.

By noon the 179th had been driven back to the final line, and the 180th was under attack from three sides by enemy tanks. The two shoulders of the salient, held by the 157th and the 180th, were only just holding their own. General Clark had arranged for air support equal to that of the day before, but overcast skies hampered operations, limiting the support to the efforts of fighter-bombers.

In midafternoon, as Colonel Darby took over the 179th Infantry, the situation was grave. An official account says that "only the 1st Battalion was capable of organized resistance." Nevertheless, General Eagles ordered Darby to hold the final line at all costs. A little later, the Germans struck with more tanks and infantry, and by 1730 fighting was intense all along the salient. Many of the 45th Division's antitank guns had been destroyed or lost in the nearly continuous action, but the GIs of the 157th and the 180th stood fast as the enemy troops and tanks pounded the shoulders of the salient. The 179th, having been reinforced by another battalion, almost miraculously was able to hold the ground. For four solid hours the Germans tried without success to break through the Allied lines east of the overpass where the 179th's 1st Battalion and the reinforcing 1st Loyals Battalion were positioned, and at one point the battle was reduced to hand-to-hand fighting.

Since the enemy had been forced to make his advances in the open, he too was taking severe losses, and at 2130 the combination of the intense Allied artillery and the determined stance of the infantry caused the enemy to pull back and regroup. The thrusts made by the green waves that night, however deep, would not be repeated. They would never again come that close to rolling up the final beachhead line.

That night the beleaguered 45th Division strengthened its positions as best it could, while Templer and Harmon were readying their forces for the counterattack the next day. The much-needed respite from attack was put to good use, and by the next morning the division had once again established mutually supporting defenses and reestablished communications between units. According to the official history, "the atmosphere of confusion and desperation which had marked the fighting during the late afternoon hours of 18 February was changing to a spirit of confidence . . ." The 45th Division had held.

All the while, the Germans were preparing for what was their last major try at cracking Lucas's final beachhead line. This time they did not wait until dawn but launched the attack at 0400, once again against the 1st Battalion of the 179th and the 1st Loyals Battalion. All morning long, German tanks and infantry tried to penetrate the defense, using the Albano road as an axis. American tank destroyers, however, helped defeat each German thrust and before noon had destroyed seven Tiger tanks. At one point a German infantry unit, supported by three tanks, actually penetrated positions of the 1st Loyals, but it was thrown back by the fire of heavy concentrations of artillery and the tank guns of one of General Harmon's regiments.

The day—19 February—was clear and warm. Plans for the corps counterattack had to be changed at the last minute because on the 18th the Germans had dropped mines in Anzio harbor, forcing a delay in the unloading of some of the equipment of the 169th Brigade. As a result, only Force H was ready to go. What was to have been a convergence of two forces at the center of the German salient was now simply a "limited-objective attack." Harmon's force got away on schedule—0630—with the 6th Armored Infantry and the 30th Regiment attacking abreast up the Bowling Alley, headed toward the center of the salient. To soften up the enemy beforehand, one of the heaviest pre-attack concentrations of artillery and air-dropped weapons to date was conducted, aided immeasurably by the cloudless day. Eight British field artillery regiments put down a supporting barrage at the LD, and eight VI Corps artillery battalions fired concentrations against suspected enemy assembly areas. Naval weapons, as well as 90-mm antiaircraft guns in direct fire, added to the destruction, as did Allied aircraft of all descriptions. According to the official history one small wooded area near the Factory was struck by 132 fighter-bombers and 48 medium bombers. . . .

At 0830 the 30th Infantry on the right and the 6th Armored on the left, having advanced together about a mile, were stopped when German resistance stiffened considerably. In the battle that ensued, the 2d Battalion, 30th Infantry, was pitted against both Tiger tanks and infantry that were lying in ambush. The battalion commander was wounded, one company was reduced to only 50 men and one officer, and another company was badly chewed up. For five hours the fight raged on, but about an hour after noon the Americans were able to renew their advance, having not only broken up the ambush but caused panic among the remaining German troops. One tank company took a group of prisoners so large that the 180th Infantry had to be called in to help with their evacuation.

By 1620 Force H had occupied the objectives assigned by VI Corps, and General Harmon called a halt to the advance, posting two battalions as a covering force. That afternoon the 1st Loyals, supported by tanks and reinforced by another British infantry company, eliminated an enemy pocket of resistance that had remained following the earlier unsuccessful German attack down Albano road. Also about this time a platoon of the 1st Armored Regiment helped the British round up another group of prisoners. The Allies then retired for the day. To Generals Clark, Lucas and Truscott, it appeared as if VI Corps had finally stopped the determined attempt by Kesselring and Mackensen to drive the Allies into the sea. General Lucas, especially, was heartened. In a message to the infantry and tankers of the Corps he said simply, "Swell work today. Keep after them."

Mackensen had been forced to commit his reserves—the 26th Panzer and 29th Panzer Grenadier Divisions—and had still been stopped. Feeble German moves on the 20th reinforced the Fifth Army and VI Corps supposition that the enemy had lost the initiative. A company attack against the 1st Loyals near the overpass was easily repulsed. German prisoners taken throughout the day reported that the scene behind their lines was one of confusion, loss of communications and suffering from the seemingly endless supply of artillery shells that rained on their positions. One prisoner recounted the story of a German battalion that

"advanced into the no man's land in the center of the salient. Under fire from all directions, the companies became confused, lost their bearings, and became hopelessly mixed up. The battalion commander called a halt to reconnoiter. He found that the 15th Panzer Grenadier Regiment, which was supposed to be on his right, was to his rear; the two connecting companies had been destroyed, and the 3d Battalion of his own regiment had failed to follow up. Left isolated and under terrific artillery fire, the battalion disintegrated."

Altogether, during the five-day attempt to dislodge the Allies the Fourteenth Army lost over 5,000 men killed, wounded or captured. Men of the 179th reported on the 21st some 500 bodies lying in front of their zone, and a recaptured American told of corpses in cordwoodlike piles—1,500 dead in all—being buried by bulldozers. Enemy prisoners recounted often that it was the continuous Allied artillery fire that "caused heavy casualties, shattered nerves, destroyed morale, and brought some units on the verge of panic." Allied aircraft, from fighters to heavy bombers, complemented the field artillery, adding immeasurably to the defeat of the Germans. Another reason cited by prisoners for their checkmate was the lack of tank support—a deficiency due both to the inability of the heavy machines to operate off the roads and to the fact that there simply were not enough of them.

Lucas's corps had paid a high price for holding the beachhead intact. The Allied casualty figure was 3,500. One factor that worsened the situation was that there was not a moment's respite for anyone in the corps. Whether they were in front or the rear mattered not; death was always near at hand. "Every man was needed," an official history says, "and the steady drain on the lives and energy of the defending troops never ceased." Even though General Lucas was a victor, he too would pay a high price. On the 22d he got the word directly from General Clark that he was to be relieved of command of the corps.

240-mm howitzer is just about to fire into German lines

General Truscott was aware that he was to become the VI Corps commander several days before Lucas himself knew that he was to be relieved. On the 18th, at the peak of the crisis at Anzio, General Clark had told Truscott that he would "probably replace Lucas within the next four or five days." Truscott replied to Clark that he was happy where he was as division commander and had no desire to relieve Lucas. Nevertheless, he said, he had not protested when Clark made him the deputy commander because "I realized that some of the command, especially on the British side, had lost confidence in Lucas." Truscott went on to say that he thought the difficulties within the command could be overcome, and that he was willing to remain as the deputy for as long as was necessary.

During the evening of 22 February, Clark told Truscott that he was to assume command of VI Corps the next day. Once again Truscott stated his objections, adding that to make such a move now, after the tactical situation had swung around to the Allied favor, "might have an unfortunate reaction on morale and undermine confidence among other officers." Lucas, Truscott observed, had a host of friends and was personally popular among American officers. There was a grave danger others might feel he was being sacrificed to British influence. According to Truscott, Clark listened to his objections, but reaffirmed his decision. The Fifth Army commander assured Truscott that Lucas would not be hurt. He would become the deputy army commander, at least for the time being. After Clark's talk with Truscott, Lucas arrived, having also been summoned, and Clark broke the bad news.

General Clark was not at all happy at having to relieve Lucas, an old friend, but had himself seen the need for a change at Anzio, over and above the pressure from Churchill and Alexander. According to Clark, his

"feeling was that Johnny Lucas was ill—tired physically and mentally— from the long responsibilities of command in battle (he died a few years later) . . . I would not under any circumstances do anything to hurt the man who had contributed so greatly to our successes since Salerno and our drive northward to Anzio."

Clark's diary concerning the situation revealed some additional thoughts, among them that he defended Lucas's initial handling of operations at the beachhead:

"Various armchair strategists in the United States and elsewhere are now [March 1944] criticizing the Fifth Army for failure to seize the Alban Hills and take Rome immediately. Such a course would have been reckless in the extreme and would have resulted in cutting off and capture by increasing enemy forces of the troops which attempted such a long advance without a secure base."

Truscott felt the same way:

"I suppose that armchair strategists will always labor under the delusion that there was a 'fleeting opportunity' at Anzio during which some Napoleonic figure would have charged over the Colli Laziali, played havoc with the German line of communications, and galloped on into Rome. Any such concept betrays lack of comprehension of the military problem involved.

. . . Under such conditions [the failure of II Corps to cross the Rapido and being in contact early on with Germans along the Anzio perimeter] any reckless drive to seize the Colli Laziali with means then available in the beachhead could only have ended in disaster and might well have resulted in destruction of the entire force."

General Marshall, after the war, commented that "for every mile of advance there were seven or more miles to be added to the perimeter," and Adleman and Walton assert that the "most superficial calculation" showed that Lucas's VI Corps base at the beachhead could never have supported such an advance. The same historians state that it was the sustained effort by Alexander that finally caused Lucas's relief. Alexander believed that Lucas, expecting an opposed landing, was not sufficiently flexible to take advantage of the lack of opposition when VI Corps set foot on the beaches, and he shared Clark's feeling that Lucas was exhausted. The army group commander knew that the situation was far from what was hoped for, and he finally remarked tellingly to General Clark, " 'We may be pushed back into the sea. That would be very bad for both of us—and you would be relieved of your command.' This gentle injunction, I am glad to say, impelled action." Long afterward General Clark told military historians that he probably made a mistake in waiting so long to take action to relieve General Lucas, but that he just wasn't able to bring himself to put this stain on his old friend's record. In any case, the change was made. Clark could no longer resist the pressure from his superiors, and Lucas lost his job.

Although Lucas was shocked when he received the news, he was not altogether surprised. According to the official history, what bothered Lucas most was that he thought he "was winning something of a victory."

Perhaps a middle-ground approach—somewhere between audacity and conservatism—would have been closer to what should have happened. Martin Blumenson, in *Anzio, the Gamble That Failed*, speaks of it this way:

"It was true that Lucas had been less than aggressive. Lucas made one serious error, and for this only he was at fault. He had failed to capture Cisterna and Campoleone when taking them would have been easy. A secure hold on these key places, Clark felt, would have given the VI Corps such a firm anchor on its beachhead that the Germans might have decided against attack."

117

Mechanical smoke generator maintains a constant screen

General Lucas served as Clark's deputy for only three weeks, after which he left Italy to command an army in the United States. The only certainty is that the question of his relief will always be subject to debate.

As is often the case when a new commander takes over, things begin to change. They did in this case, subtly, with General Truscott now at the helm. Truscott himself admitted that he did things differently from Lucas's way. This began with his behavior at the front. Where Lucas most often stayed in his wine-cellar command post, Truscott was out with the infantry much of the time. An imposing figure, Truscott projected an image of confidence that soon radiated throughout the corps. Before long, says Blumenson, "an intangible feeling of hope took hold of the Allied troops."

In spite of the VI Corps success, there was no time to rest, because Kesselring and Mackensen were determined to try once again, as soon as they could regroup. On 22 February, for example, the combat strength of the German 65th Infantry Division was only 673 men; similar problems existed elsewhere in the Fourteenth Army, and there was no question that it would have to reorganize itself before it could make another effort to oust the British and Americans. The only choice open to the Germans, the only place where they could reasonably expect to be successful, was against the 3d Division at Cisterna. This was Mackensen's recommended course of action.

Truscott, too, knew that he had little time to reconstitute his battered corps. He moved the command post out of the "gloomy" wine cellar and took positive steps to improve the coordination of the artillery fire, ruffling the feathers of a few high-ranking Allied officers in the process. As for the soldiers along the beachhead perimeter, they too were moved about somewhat. Beginning before Lucas left, on 19 February, the 6th Armored Infantry, less a battalion, was withdrawn to the rear and placed in corps reserve. This move was to enable it to support the 180th Infantry, which was holding the right shoulder of the German salient. On 22 February a battalion of the 30th Infantry reverted to 3d Division control and was put in line between the 45th and 3d Divisions. At the same time the 45th Division front was shortened by a mile as the boundary line was moved west from Carano. These changes, in effect, materially strengthened the 180th Regiment's sector.

As for the left shoulder of the salient, responsibility was given totally to the 1st and 56th Divisions. The 2d and 3d Battalions of the 157th, both of which had borne much of the German onslaught, were relieved by units of the two British divisions. Both of these shifts of units served to halve the 45th Division front, and General Eagles wasted no time in regrouping, resupplying and resting his exhausted troops. Although a rotation policy was begun, and some replacements were received, the 1st and 56th Divisions were so severely understrength that Truscott deemed their general situation to be critical. VI Corps strongly urged General Clark to send reinforcements over and above the 18th Brigade, which had already arrived at Anzio and been attached to the 1st Division, partially relieving the British manpower problem. Additional fresh troops, however, would not be forthcoming until early in March.

The Allies had little intelligence concerning the area in front of the 3d Division, but patrols on the night of the 27th detected more than the usual enemy presence. Late on the 28th, behind a smokescreen, the Germans

Major General
John W. O'Daniel
(later picture)

made final preparations for their attack. Suspecting that something was up, the 3d Division called for a massive artillery barrage to its front, to begin at dawn on the 29th. Twice the size of any Allied artillery concentration to date—including the height of the crisis—it slowed but failed to halt the enemy attack. The worst penetration, and the only really serious one, was in the sector held by the 509th Parachute Battalion on the division left. One of its companies was nearly destroyed—only 23 men survived—but the rest of the battalion managed to stop the enemy drive.

For two days the Germans, using the heavily reinforced 362d Division, tried repeatedly to push through the center of the 3d Division defense, only to be repulsed each time. During the morning of the 29th, cloud cover and rain prevented Allied close air support, but that afternoon the weather cleared sufficiently to allow the MAAF to assist in the fray. Although the 3d Division took heavy losses, it counterattacked strongly on 1 March. So successful was the American stance that Truscott said to General O'Daniel he was "delighted with the way you have stopped the Boche." On 2 March the Allied air forces struck the Germans in earnest with 241 B-24s and 100 B-17s—almost 200 P-38s and P-47s were in escort—and effectively put an end to the German drive. Unknown to Clark and Truscott, this event marked the last day there would ever be a major German assault against the infantrymen at Anzio.

9. Respite

A brief but dramatic description by Bill Mauldin conveys the desperate situation faced by VI Corps during the last days of February 1944. "The Krauts launched a suicidal attack which almost drove through to the sea," he wrote. "Evacuation was already beginning in the harbor when a single American battalion broke the point of the attack, then was engulfed and died." He continued, "Bodies of fanatical young Germans piled up in front of the machine guns, and when the guns ran out of ammunition the Wehrmacht came through and was stopped only by point-blank artillery." Hitler had ordered the Allies eliminated and his loyal followers would pay any price to do it. The prestige of the German Army—at home and abroad—demanded the extermination of the American and British toehold at Anzio. Survive the Allies did, but beginning in March, both sides—exhausted, depleted and badly in need of supplies of every kind—stood in place for a period of relative quiet.

The German high command committed to the battle everything it dared—and failed. Why? Some ascribed the failure to the fighting spirit and will to win of the individual Allied infantryman. Although this was part of it, there was more. Mauldin stated, "One American artillery battalion of 155's fired 80,000 rounds of ammunition at Anzio and there were dozens of these battalions." General von Mackensen later said that 75 percent of all wounds his soldiers sustained were caused by shell fragments. Artillery was also responsible for the wreck of communications and supply facilities, not to mention the effect on morale. The survival of the Anzio beachhead was, undoubtedly, the result of a combination of factors.

Numbers of ingenious devices were developed during and after the intensive fighting of January and February. Tanks were equipped with cranes to retrieve other damaged or stalled armor. A "mangle buggy" was a mechanism, made of jeep parts, which trailed a primer cord. It was aimed at barbed wire where it thrashed its way in, then detonated to clear a passage for troops. General O'Daniel was credited with inventing the battle sled, a portable foxhole drawn along behind a tank. The infantryman in this shallow metal dish was supposed to get close enough to seize his objective. In practice the sleds caught on ravines or the edges of holes and were vulnerable to mines and shell fragments. A harpoon-firing mortar was successful in clearing antipersonnel mines. When it was discharged the harpoon stuck in the ground and the trailing primer cord ignited to clear away obstacles for attacking troops. A pipe filled with TNT and shoved into a minefield worked much the same way. These pipes were often connected together to form "snakes" as much as 100 feet long. When the TNT was detonated by tank machine gun fire, the resulting explosion was strong enough to touch off mines five feet deep and clear a space large enough for a tank to pass through.

The U.S. First Special Service Force was uniquely in its element at this time. Its 1,600 men were at one point responsible for almost a third of the perimeter. Besides the ordinary duties involved in guarding their piece of Italy, they indulged in extracurricular activities for which they had been meticulously trained. At night they infiltrated enemy lines, slitting the throats of any Germans they found. They would then add a note of terror by leaving a sticker on a victim's helmet warning his comrades, "You May Be Next!" Not content to steal chickens, wine and the like from the Germans, they actually set up a base of operations behind enemy lines and farmed the countryside when they were not patrolling.

Allied artillery was especially efficient through use of a system called TOT (Time On Target), developed first by General Penney. It consisted, simply, of concentrated fire into a single German position. General Truscott described it thus: "Each division selected the most profitable target on its front. At specific times, every gun within range was brought to bear for three rounds of TOT, for which firing data had been computed so that all projectiles exploded on the target at the same instant." The result was devastating against German artillery and tank concentrations and disrupted potential counterattacks.

Shorter-range enemy artillery positions were often neutralized when the TOT system decimated each battery immediately after it opened fire.

General Truscott brings new vigor to the VI Corps command

Long-range guns were another thing. The Anzio Express, a common term designating the German 210- and 280-mm railway guns, continued to bombard the entire beachhead. Air strikes against these guns were only moderately successful. The big guns, fired for only 10 minutes and then moved to other sites or rolled into railroad tunnels, caused many of the casualties and much of the damage to supplies in the congested harbor.

Newly developed radar (called SCR 584) was instrumental in solving the problem of Luftwaffe attacks. Radar-directed and -controlled antiaircraft guns made high-level bombing a dangerous affair. In many cases German bombing missions were broken up even before they reached the beachhead, but when the enemy then concentrated on low-level bombing, other defensive steps had to be taken. The beachhead was divided into five sectors and the guns deployed to cover all air space within each one. As enemy planes entered one sector, all others were alerted. The guns of the sector under attack would then fire six rounds at a prescribed rate, repeating the volley on order as long as the aircraft was in their area. This system—plus the radar-controlled batteries—virtually ended German air attacks.

123

But in spite of the innovations, fierce fighting continued along the 21-mile perimeter of the beachhead, and there were plenty of opportunities for heroism. A Medal of Honor was earned by Sergeant John C. Squires when, near Padiglione, he came under fire for the first time. Reconnoitering an area to ascertain the effect of enemy artillery on the troops, he was able to reroute his platoon, gather stragglers and lost men into another platoon and establish an outpost on a small creek. Twice he braved intense fire and minefields to bring up reinforcements. Fighting off repeated counterattacks, he captured a German Spandau machine gun and turned it on its former owners. Then, attacking enemy machine guns south of his position, he captured 21 Germans and 13 more Spandau guns. Using these weapons, he and his men fought off another enemy attack the next night. Although Squires survived this experience, he was killed in action later in the campaign.

The static condition of the perimeter allowed one of the logistic miracles of the war to take place. As was obvious to all concerned during the planning stages of Shingle, resupply was the crucial element at Anzio. General Clark's conditions were more than met, however, because Anzio became the fourth largest seaport in the world during March 1944. After it became obvious that there would be no early linkup with Allied forces to the south, supply plans had to be revised. A maximum of six LSTs could dock at Anzio's harbor at one time; consequently, six of them left Naples every day at 1700. They arrived at Anzio at 0600 the following morning, and their 151 tons each was unloaded. Of the cargo, 60 percent was ammunition, 20 percent fuel and 20 percent rations. Liberty ships arrived at 10-day intervals. Because of the shallowness of the harbor, they had to anchor two miles offshore and were unloaded by LSTs or, in calm weather, DUKWs. LCIs were used mostly as personnel carriers.

Anzio harbor—limited room for LSTs

Initially VI Corps had the responsibility for the organization of supply and evacuation. The beach party consisted of the 540th Engineer Combat Regiment, along with accompanying Army and Navy personnel, and numbered about 4,200 men. Administration of the harbor was assumed by the Fifth Army in mid-February. An entire port battalion, the 488th, was sent to Anzio to discharge cargo, moving from ship to ship and averaging over 1,000 tons a day in spite of air attacks, long-range guns and E-boats. But, owing both to casualties and to the lack of suitable equipment for unloading heavy items, efficiency was not as high as it might have been. This problem was solved by putting aboard each LST or Liberty ship a contingent of troops plus rations and proper gear with which to discharge the cargo. Once the job was done, the men and gear returned to Naples and another group took the next trip. Since the faster the cargo was unloaded, the sooner the men could get out of Anzio, they worked doubly hard, and the amount of tonnage unloaded went up. From 6 February to the 29th, 73,000 tons was discharged, but in March, under the new arrangement, more than twice that amount was unloaded. On 29 March a record of almost 8,000 tons of unloaded cargo was reached. According to one source, "by May 23 the beachhead had, in addition to the usual ten-day reserve, a full month's additional reserve of supplies."

Once supplies were on the beach, it was the job of the men of the Quartermaster Corps to keep them from being destroyed by enemy fire before they were needed at the front. At first there was much destruction, because each hit would sympathetically set off other explosions among the piles of ammunition and gasoline drums. A method of protection was devised similar to that used for the hospital. Supplies were divided into smaller dumps, and earth was piled around the sides. This effort did not protect the dump from direct hits, but it did lessen the chance of a chain reaction. It was especially effective in the gasoline dumps because the berms kept air away from the fuel, cutting down on the number of fires. A homemade bulldozer was used to push earth from the revetment over any fires that did develop, smothering them.

Between early March and late May the stalemate between VI Corps and the Fourteenth Army produced a unique atmosphere and way of life for the thousands of Allied soldiers at Anzio. They seemed to be living on an island rather than in a beachhead. It was their home for months. Things could have been worse, but perhaps not much. Thousands of men, and the supplies to support them, were confined in a "small, pie-shaped sector," as General Clark described it, under the constant observation of the enemy, who held the high ground inland. Bill Mauldin described the situation very clearly: "You wondered how Jerry could see you and throw a shell at you every time you stuck your head up, until you climbed into the mountains after it was all over and were able to count every tree and every house in the area we had held." The reclaimed marshland and rolling

Supply dump holds a 60-day supply of B, K and other rations

farmland offered little cover from small arms fire and none from artillery. The slight rise in the land behind the beaches provided the best shelter, but it was usually inadequate.

Ernie Pyle, in his book *Brave Men,* observed that "the most indiscriminate shell dropped at any point on the beachhead would have landed not more than two hundred yards from somebody. And the average shell found thousands within hearing distance of its explosion." There was no rear area to rest in, no rear echelon, no place to safely unload the thousands of tons of supplies. "A man was just as liable to get his standing in the doorway of the villa where he slept at night as he was in a command post five miles out in the field." Mauldin agreed:

> "Sometimes it was worse at the front; sometimes worse at the harbor. Quartermasters buried their dead and amphibious duck drivers went down with their craft. Infantrymen dug into the Mussolini Canal, had the canal pushed in on top of them by armor-piercing shells, and Jerry bombers circled as they directed glider bombs into LSTs and Liberty ships. Wounded men got Oak Leaf Clusters on their Purple Hearts when shell fragments riddled them as they lay on hospital beds."

Doctors, nurses and patients died when long-range artillery—and bombers—missed their targets. Placed in a particularly open area where the Red Cross symbol could be seen, they were vulnerable to any enemy fire directed at the harbor and beach. General Truscott remembered the hospital situation: "More than one [wounded man] said to me: 'General, get us out of here. Let us go back to the front. We are better off there than here.'" Truscott, appreciative of the gallant effort of the medical personnel, men and women, under such extreme conditions, resolved to do something about the situation. The 36th Engineers (later reinforced with details from the 3d Infantry) began digging in the hospital. Because the water table was so high in this area, they could go down only two feet. Sandbags were filled and stacked to provide walls to a height of four feet. Operating rooms were given timber and sandbagged roofs, though wards were covered only with canvas. The wounded men's cots, since they were below ground level, were safe from anything but a direct hit.

The hospital was not the only thing dug in. Living underground became the mode of life for nearly everyone behind the front lines. An average dugout was a square or rectangular hole in the sandy soil, employing lumber, bedsprings or similar items to keep the sides from caving in. Ceilings were made of timbers, boards or doors and covered with soil, making them almost invulnerable to the shelling. The closer to the beaches they were, the more elaborate these shelters became. Boredom and ingenuity combined to produce impressive innovations. Bill Mauldin described them in *Up Front:*

> "Some blossomed out with reading lamps made from salvaged jeep headlights and batteries, and a few huts had wooden floors and real rugs and charcoal stoves made from German gas cans and the flexible tubing that had been used to waterproof vehicles for the landing. Old brass from shells made good stove parts, and the thick cardboard shell cases were used to line walls and to make 'sidewalks' through the mud."

Although incoming shells continued to wound and kill, the dugouts proved to be effective in holding casualties to a minimum. "It was only the first shell after a lull that got many casualties," wrote Pyle. However, he added later, "it was an unusual day when somebody wasn't killed within their own little village of dugouts." Bill Mauldin once got into trouble by drawing a cartoon about a real MP who, very wisely, directed traffic from a hole near his duty station. When criticized by the MPs, Mauldin retorted: "That was no gag. Crossroads are good places to stay in holes—especially Anzio crossroads."

General Truscott had moved his command post from underground to a small wine shop. The rest of the headquarters remained in the wine cellar, which was hard to leave once you got down there, according to Mauldin.

"It wasn't only a good place to stay away from shells. Many of the little niches had big vino barrels."

Truscott's wine shop was one of the rare instances in which the existing buildings of Anzio afforded protection. When the troops had landed on D-day, they found the city deserted but intact. As time passed and the artillery rounds fell, Anzio was gradually reduced to rubble. Ernie Pyle wrote that

"a few buildings would go down, or the corners would fly off some of them. One day's damage was almost negligible. But the cumulative effect after a couple of weeks was heartbreaking. . . . Broken steel girders lay across the sidewalks. Marble statues fell in littered patios. Trees were uprooted, and the splattered mud upon them dried and turned gray. Wreckage was washed up on shore. Everywhere there were rubble and mud and broken wire."

Along the perimeter the troops had only shallow foxholes for protection. Water rose in holes only two feet deep, and overhead protection of some kind was needed against shell fragments. Rain, snow and confinement added to the discomfort of the men who had to live in these water-filled ruts for days at a time. The wounded could be removed only at night and had to hang on until then under these same conditions. One result of the constant dampness was trench foot. Dry socks arrived periodically but were wet in a few minutes. Ernie Pyle noted that a use for the brushless shaving cream issued to the troops was as a preventive for trench foot. Another malady he commented on was known as "Nettuno neurosis" or "Anzio anxiety." "Anzio foot" was described as the feet walking in one direction and the body diving for protection in another. "Anzio walk" was a series of twists, jerks and ducks—the way a man walks who is under constant shellfire. Although the men joked about the nervous tension, it was real enough—and many succumbed to it.

There was a standing joke between American and British troops. The Americans, with their overwhelming amounts of material, were rather wasteful of it—especially in the eyes of the British, who had had to conserve for many years. Piles of discarded equipment were strewn about, and when a British unit relieved an American one the Tommies berated the GIs for leaving a "messy battlefield."

Training, necessitated by the number of replacements arriving, continued during this "quiet" period. The best method for the integration of these fresh troops was to pull a unit out of the line and back into the rest- and training-camp area. There the new men could get acquainted with the veterans and undergo a few days of training. Replacements thrown into the line without this period spent their first hours of combat lacking the comfort of comradeship. Ernie Pyle understood what this meant: "To go up to the brink of possible death in the night-time in a faraway land, puzzled and

Landing craft conveys wounded men to a hospital ship in Anzio bay

afraid, knowing no one, and facing the worst moment of your life totally alone—that takes strength."

In spite of the grim circumstances—the problems of supply and the constant shelling—the cooks did their imaginative best to enhance their limited menus. Some help was received from the local livestock. Many instances of bovine suicide were noted, and the sacrifices did not go in vain. Ernie Pyle claimed that "we saw an occasional cow deliberately walk up and stick her head in front of a rifle just as it went off." Regulations against eating these unfortunate suicides were ignored: K rations were no match for fresh meat when you had a choice. Germans sometimes drove cattle before them during an attack, and one American soldier declared that he had killed a Nazi cow in self-defense when it attacked him. Naturally, he ate it. The food exchange between American and British troops was brisk— American 10-in-1 for bully beef. Other delicacies were chickens, rabbits and fish. The men of the Special Service Force found their own way to add fish to their diet. They used German antitank mines, rewired electrically and detonated under water, to stun or kill the fish. Then it was just a matter of picking them up.

In spite of the addition of an occasional chicken, fish or piece of beef, Allied soldiers continued to gripe about the monotony of the daily fare. One GI, who had been captured and then had escaped, reported to his buddies that the Germans had fed him three meals a day plus "a chocolate bar, ten cigarettes and a bottle of beer." Bill Mauldin reflected that perhaps it was a Nazi plot to demoralize the American troops. "If the Krauts fed him like that and then deliberately let him escape, it was a smart trick."

British troops were given a liquor ration—evoking envy on the part of the American soldiers. Distilleries appeared, made of gasoline cans and tubing from wrecked airplanes. The product was called Kickapoo Joy Juice and, according to one authority, "wasn't bad stuff when you cut it with canned grapefruit juice." Eventually, the American troops received beer brought in from a rebuilt brewery in Naples.

One unexpected luxury at Anzio was the bakery. Eighty soldier-bakers worked, under fire, to produce around 2,700 pounds of bread per day.

Aside from eating and drinking there were other forms of recreation at Anzio. Games were popular, especially card games. There were also volleyball, badminton and, of course, baseball. Ball games were usually played in areas close to shelter from artillery. General Truscott recalled that "it was not unusual to see softball games in progress with German artillery shells landing within five or six hundred yards." A joke about one particular game was popular. Along the Mussolini Canal both armies were content to maintain what was, relatively speaking, an uneasy peace, and this area was favored for baseball games. The joke goes that during one game the umpire called a man out at home on a particularly close play. From across the canal came the shout, "Whaddayuh mean, out? He vas safe a mile, ya bum!"

As the weather permitted, the men went swimming and water skiing, using a DUKW as a ski-boat, in the Tyrrhenian Sea. There were two underground theaters, and division bands were brought up from Naples to play concerts throughout the area. British bagpipe bands were also very popular. And the "Anzio Derby" and the "Beachhead Preakness" were horse and mule races staged by the troops which were complete with public address systems and a 12-piece band. One area was set aside for a rest camp. Although it was like every other place at Anzio, under fire, it did afford a change of scene for the men on the tension-ridden front lines. Ernie Pyle quotes one soldier as saying, "There's a hell of a difference between getting shells spasmodically at long range and being right up under Jerry's nose where he's aiming at you personally." Regularly a group of 750 men left by LST for a few days in Naples.

Homemade radios were abundant. Since Allied programs could be picked up only by the more sophisticated receivers, the most popular program was the Germans' Axis Sally. This propaganda broadcast included the latest popular music from the United States. General Clark felt that the broadcasts were a dangerous influence, but most of the troops considered

German prisoners are herded into an LST

the propaganda a source of amusement. Sally's theme song, "Lili Marlene," became a favorite of the Americans, as it had earlier been for the British Tommies in Africa.

General Truscott, always appreciative of the courage and tenacity of his troops, wrote:

> "I shall always admire the trait in men and women who served there which prompted them always to seek relaxation in the normal pastimes of peacetime living, reminding them of home. Without this I do not see how men could have survived the terrific nervous tensions under which they lived at Anzio."

"When you weren't getting something you were expecting something," Mauldin explained. The sense of vulnerability and confinement were constant, and Axis Sally gleefully described the beachhead as "the largest self-supporting prisoner-of-war camp in the world."

At Anzio, besides replacements for troops already there, a number of changes took place among VI Corps units. The British 5th Division arrived to replace the depleted 56th. The 1st Division remained with some minor reorganization. Among the American units the Rangers and the paratroopers left. The 504th Parachute Infantry joined the 82d Airborne Division in the United Kingdom in late March. The next month the 509th Parachute Infantry Battalion was withdrawn. Arriving in April was the 34th Division, relieving the 3d Division, which had been on the front line for 67 consecutive days. The 3d Division was placed in corps reserve. By the end of March, VI Corps outnumbered the opposing Fourteenth Army. Some thought and planning was given to initiating a new offensive, but owing mostly to problems on the southern front, it was at first postponed, then canceled altogether.

Along the Gustav Line, German and Allied armies faced each other in a stalemate similar to that at Anzio, only in reverse. Here it was the Germans who were dug in, repulsing attack after attack by the Allied forces. German soldiers, however, lived in dugouts constructed of steel and concrete. General Clark tells of one example. "We found out later that during one of our intense bombing and artillery attacks—an attack in which we threw all the great weight our forces could muster against a comparatively small target area—a group of German officers sat in an underground bunker in the mountainside playing cards."

The equivalent of four German divisions manned the southern front, skillfully using the natural terrain to stymie the advance of six Allied divisions. After the attempt in February to take Monte Cassino, General Alexander decided he would need a superiority of three to one to overcome the enemy's resistance. To accomplish this he shifted U.S. Fifth Army to cover the sector from the Tyrrhenian Sea to the Liri Valley, while the British Eighth Army took the Liri and Cassino front and received control of McCreery's X (British) Corps.

This reorganization also accomplished the grouping of diverse nationalities according to the origin of their equipment. Under the Fifth Army was the French Expeditionary Corps of General Juin; it had been supplied with American weapons and equipment while in North Africa. British-equipped Dominion, Indian, Polish and other troops were included in the Eighth Army. North of the Eighth Army was the British V Corps, holding territory from the eastern slope of the Apennines to the Adriatic coast, under the direct control of Headquarters, AAI.

This massive realignment of forces was carried on mostly by night. The Polish corps, however, found it necessary to continue movement by day, and constructed miles of camouflage to shield the roadways. Dummy tanks and trucks were placed to cover the withdrawal of some units, and the noise of nighttime movement was covered by artillery fire.

Meanwhile, the Mediterranean Allied Air Force carried out operation Strangle, a series of air attacks against road, rail and sea routes serving the Germans. Although Strangle succeeded in interdicting lines of communication to and from Rome and in the battle area, the interruptions to the flow of German men and matériel were only temporary. It was not able to isolate the battlefield, as had been hoped.

The main offensive during March was the attack by the New Zealanders on the town of Cassino. After three hours of intensive bombing, the artillery continued to soften up the defense, and Allied forces moved for-

240-mm howitzer is dug in and camouflaged

ward. Enemy casualties were high, but the German troops rallied and, using the newly created rubble for barricades, caused the attacking New Zealand troops to pay heavily for the part of the town they captured. General Clark remarked that "their [German] counterattacks frequently regained scattered key points that we had taken at high sacrifice." By 23 March the New Zealand Corps had suffered 1,594 casualties, but the Germans still held a portion of Cassino town as well as Monte Cassino.

General Alexander's guidelines for the coming offensive were simple. The Eighth Army was to take the rest of the town of Cassino, as well as Monte Cassino, and then push up the Liri Valley. The Fifth Army was to fight through the Aurunci Mountains, threatening the flank of the German positions in the Liri and at the same time assuring safe use of Highway 7 along the coast. VI Corps would break out of the beachhead, attacking eastward to cut off the enemy routes of retreat and then, turning south, catch the German Tenth Army in a pincer.

To throw the Germans off guard, a plan (Nunton) was worked out to convince them that the Allies were going to make an amphibious landing at Civitavecchia, north of Rome. To add to the credibility of the fake landing, the 36th Division was sent to an area near Naples to receive more amphibious training. Canadian troops were dispatched to help in the delusion, and reconnaissance missions were ordered for the Civitavecchia area. The German command, convinced that the Allied armies along the Gustav and in the Anzio pocket could not break through the entrenched German lines, were ready to buy the idea of an amphibious assault above Rome. The scheme was a complete success.

133

10. Diadem

The respite—or stalemate—lasted more than two months. It was not until 11 May that the Allies were once again ready to try to get the two armies, the Fifth and the Eighth, connected and advance northward to Rome. Although the time of waiting was frustrating to the British and American commanders, the infantrymen along the Gustav Line and inside the perimeter at Anzio enjoyed the early spring of 1944. As the troops welcomed the sunshine, General Alexander's planners were busying themselves, in the greatest secrecy, with the planning for Diadem, as the spring offensive was code-named. There were two major goals underpinning this operation. The first and, at least to some individuals, the most important was the capture of Rome. The second, just as important to overall Allied strategy but the less glamorous of the two, was to keep as many German divisions as possible busy in the Italian theater, so that they could not be used against the Allies in Overlord, only weeks away.

Generals Clark and Alexander were never quite in agreement as to how the Allies should proceed. Early in the Allied planning, before the stalemate, Clark saw Anzio as an adjunct to the main attack at Cassino; it would pin down German forces at the beachhead to preclude their use along the Gustav Line. Alexander believed, to the contrary, that it would be Anzio that compelled the Germans to withdraw from Cassino, and that the two thrusts—at Anzio and up the Liri—would catch the Germans in a trap south of Rome. In discussing Diadem, Alexander drew an analogy to boxing, saying that the Fifth and Eighth Armies along the southern front would throw the first punch. Then VI Corps would strike out with a hook from the Anzio beachhead. Alexander's basic purpose, to trap the Germans, had not changed. He had decided, however, that the Eighth Army would now be the force along the Gustav Line that had the major role—to advance up the Liri Valley to Valmontone, where it would join VI Corps after the breakout. Information from the Ultra intelligence operation had provided positive knowledge that Valmontone was a particularly weak point in the German defenses. While the Eighth Army made its move, the Fifth Army, along the Garigliano, was to turn the enemy flank in the south, driving up the coast to Anzio. Valmontone, rather than Rome, was to be the initial and major focal point during Diadem.

The realignment of forces dictated by General Alexander during the respite had left the Fifth Army with a smaller front—Anzio and part of the Gustav Line—and a total of seven American, four French and two British divisions. At the beachhead, General Clark had the two British and about three and a half U.S. divisions. From the mouth of the Garigliano to the Liri River, the Fifth Army fielded the 36th and 85th Divisions on line, and the 88th in reserve, all under II Corps; and the FEC with the 3d Algerian, 2d Moroccan, 4th Mountain and the Italian 1st Motorized Divisions.

North of the Fifth Army, Alexander positioned the Eighth Army, with three corps, on a relatively short front extending from the Liri to the northern slope of the Apennines. The British V Corps held the line from the Apennines to the Adriatic Sea. From south to north along the Gustav Line in the Eighth Army sector were British XIII Corps, II Polish Corps and British X Corps. This formidable force was the one that was called upon in Diadem to make the main attack to the northwest.

Field Marshal Kesselring expected an Allied attack somewhere, but the German high command was compelled, because of commitments elsewhere, to leave the Tenth and Fourteenth Armies to their own resources. In spite of Operation Strangle, Kesselring's two armies had experienced an increase in troop strength of about 30,000 men. In addition to the 23 divisions on hand on 1 May, Kesselring also had troops attached from the Luftwaffe and the Waffen SS: all in all, the German ground strength totaled just over 400,000 men. The respite had been put to good use by the Germans. Because of reorganization, the use of Italian labor and the rest and rehabilitation enjoyed by some of the best divisions, the Commander in Chief South (OB SÜD) had forces that were superior in quality to German units elsewhere.

The deception plan, Nunton, that Alexander had set in motion during the stalemate, as well as a number of other factors, caused confusion among

Field Marshal Sir Harold Alexander (others not identified)

Kesselring's intelligence analysts as to what, exactly, the Allies would do when they attacked. Because there were two fronts south of Rome, OB SÜD had to have reserves readily available to both areas. Since the deception had helped convince the Germans of the vulnerability of the coast both north and south of Anzio, they wanted to have mobile units on hand in case anything happened along the Tyrrhenian Sea. Kesselring was also concerned about an airborne landing near Frosinone; he therefore had to put one of his divisions nearby. Preparing for all these contingencies required that he separate his forces more than he liked. As for aircraft and aircrews, the Germans were woefully lacking. The Americans and the British could field some 4,000 aircraft, but the Luftwaffe had only 700 operational aircraft in the central Mediterranean area. Of this number, less than half were based in Italy.

General Alexander had reserved for himself the decision as to when VI Corps would make the breakout and head toward Valmontone. The timing depended entirely on the progress of the Fifth Army units and the Eighth Army on the southern front. Actually, VI Corps would not jump off until 23 May.

Diadem began on the 11th with an artillery barrage of the greatest magnitude. Nearly 1,000 guns in the Cassino area were trained on targets that had been carefully selected during the previous weeks; almost 174,000 rounds were fired during the first 24 hours of the battle. MAAF, in what was actually a continuation of Operation Strangle, supported the attack with fighter-bomber strikes against numerous key German positions along the defensive line. According to General Clark, the barrage "was perhaps the most effective artillery bombardment of the campaign. It simply smashed into dust a great number of enemy batteries and vital centers . . . For hours . . . they were still confused and unable to establish good centralized direction of their defense lines."

Commonwealth, Polish, French, Italian and American troops began their assault in unison after the artillery had done its work. II Polish Corps made a determined attack against Monte Cassino, which after attempts by various forces had yet to be captured, and it too was unsuccessful. The Poles lost so much equipment and so many men that after 12 hours of the bloodiest fighting they had to refit and regroup for three days before they could try again. At the entrance to the Liri Valley, the British did get across the Rapido. Vietinghoff's defenders put up such stiff opposition that XIII Corps, three days later, had barely expanded its bridgehead into the valley itself. It was the Fifth Army, not the Eighth, that finally broke the Gustav Line, and it was the French, not the Americans of II Corps. Along the Garigliano, General Keyes and his II Corps—using the relatively newly arrived 85th and 88th Divisions, the first in the theater to be comprised mostly of draftees—made little progress in spite of three days of bitter fighting.

The FEC, under the able direction of General Juin, pushed forward for a solid 24 hours in unbridled attack and drove the Germans from the rugged mountains northwest of the Garigliano. On the 13th, General Juin's trained mountain fighters were overlooking the Liri Valley from the southern heights, actually several miles west of Cassino, having finished what General Clark considered to be "one of the most brilliant and daring advances of the war in Italy." By 16 May the FEC had reached Monte Revole, and the remainder of its units were slanted back to maintain contact with the Eighth Army. General Clark later extolled the FEC in the following terms.

> "Only the most careful preparations and the utmost determination made this attack possible, but Juin was that kind of fighter. Mule pack trains, skilled mountain fighters, and men with the strength to make long night marches through treacherous terrain were needed to succeed in the all-but-impregnable mountain ranges.
>
> The French displayed that ability during their sensational advance which Lieutenant General Siegfried Westphal, the chief of staff to Kesselring, later described as a major battle surprise both in timing and aggressiveness. For this performance, which was to be a key to the success of the entire drive on Rome, I shall always be a grateful admirer of General Juin and his magnificent FEC."

By 15 May the British were able to start up the Liri Valley, having expanded their bridgehead considerably in four days of fighting. XIII Corps had gone against the best defenses the Germans had to offer, and during those four days had suffered more than 4,000 casualties. On the 18th the Polish 3d Carpathian Division finally took Monte Cassino and the abbey,

Ruined Cassino abbey is finally surrendered by the Germans

now mostly rubble. The fall of Monte Cassino was the culmination of almost half a year of efforts to crack the Gustav Line. This particular piece of Italy, including the town below, which fell the same day, had been the scene of some of the bitterest fighting in the campaign. Americans, Commonwealth troops and the Poles had tried, and finally the last had been successful. According to General Clark, the Polish soldiers had "fought with utter bravery and disregard for casualties" until finally achieving victory.

Before the Allied assault was four days old, Kesselring knew he was in trouble. Not only had Allied aircraft damaged a considerable portion of his communications and virtually destroyed Tenth Army headquarters, but the front was crumbling on all sides. On the 16th, he decided that without reinforcements his southern forces would surely lose, and he ordered one of his best divisions, the 29th Panzer Grenadiers, which was at that point near Anzio, to reinforce the Tenth Army. Additionally, Kesselring alerted Mackensen that more troops would possibly be needed soon.

By the time the 29th Division arrived, it was too late. The FEC had already gone 10 miles to the northwest and had actually penetrated what was called the Hitler Line, another German defensive position. The situation for the Tenth Army was bad and getting rapidly worse. Two German colonels, discussing their predicament, summarized it tersely.

BEELITZ: "Jesus Christ, I doubted that the enemy would be that strong."

WENTZELL: "You don't know the French colonial troops. They are a bunch of roughnecks. Life means nothing to them."

Kesselring had another good reserve division near Anzio, the 26th

138

34th Division GIs operate a mortar

Panzer Grenadiers. He finally committed it also, but to no avail. The Allied advance proceeded. Two German divisions had nearly been destroyed—the 71st, by the FEC, and the 94th, which had been opposing II Corps.

By 19 May the French had made their way some 20 miles northwest of the Garigliano and crossed the Itri-Pico road, one of the main lateral highways connecting Highways 6 and 7 south of Rome. On that same day the coastal town of Gaeta fell to the Americans.

With the situation now highly favorable for the Allies, the time had come to decide just when VI Corps should attempt to make its breakout from the long-established perimeter at Anzio. How to use these divisions was a matter of some dispute between the two Allied generals most directly responsible for the conduct of the Italian campaign, Alexander and Clark. Events leading to the decision did not follow one another in what could be considered routine military fashion, but they nevertheless were eventually to result in VI Corps beginning what would be its most successful maneuver. This would occur about the same time as the Allies captured Terracina and Pico.

The Americans and the French were at this point well on their way to seizing these two villages. Fondi, almost eight miles north of Itri, fell to the Americans on the 20th. The French were at that time advancing on Pico, the capture of which might trap the Tenth Army in the Liri Valley. On the 21st, an American battalion, in a small amphibious maneuver using DUKWs as assault craft, left Gaeta and landed at Sperlonga unopposed. The battalion had actually been heading for Terracina, but the DUKWs were inadequate for the seas, literally forcing the unit to take Sperlonga instead. In any case, Terracina, 10 miles up the coast, and Pico were within reach. On this same day, General Clark ordered General Truscott to begin his own attack on 23 May.

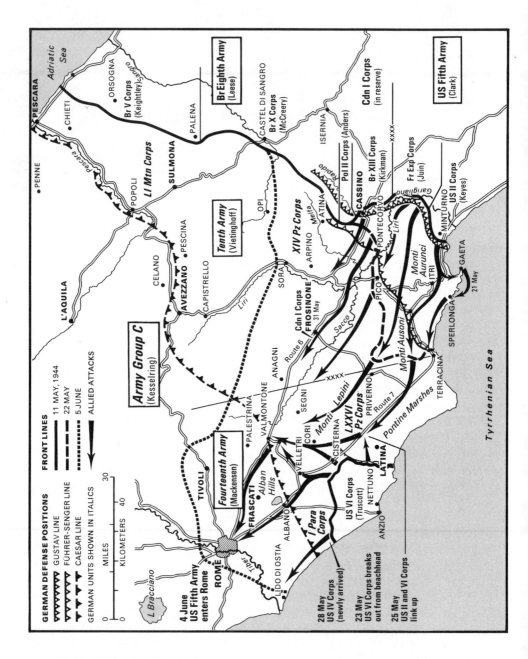

ANZIO—THE FINAL PHASES

11. Eruption from the Beachhead

Newspapers in the United States were confidently reporting Allied progress on the southern front as the time drew near for VI Corps to make its move at Anzio. The Newark *Evening News,* for one, announced that the "battle lines moved nearer Rome"; the New York *Times* in a somewhat mistaken but nevertheless vivid account said that "German defenses along two-thirds of the blazing Hitler Line [*sic*] battleground from the Liri River to the Tyrrhenian Sea crumbled before American and French attacks today, with Gaeta abandoned to the Allies in a disorganized Nazi retreat that approached the proportions of a rout." On 24 May the *Times* proclaimed the two fronts "now aflame in central Italy." The last declaration was true, insofar as General Truscott's infantrymen were concerned, for one day earlier they had indeed made their move.

To the men of the VI Corps planning staff, the beginning of the breakout did not mean the culmination of the relatively smooth planning cycle that accompanies a coordinated infantry attack. VI Corps was supposed to head directly for Valmontone, but there was doubt as to just exactly what would happen, and the reason for this doubt was political.

Although General Alexander had stayed with his basic plan to trap the German Tenth Army behind the Gustav Line, General Clark during April had begun to wonder about the total situation. Alexander's regrouping of the armies along the Gustav Line had put the Eighth Army rather than the Fifth on the probable axis to Rome. With this point in mind, Clark began to change his thoughts about VI Corps at the beachhead. Perhaps he could capitalize on the proximity of Anzio to Rome by having Truscott break out and go directly north to the Alban Hills and then win the race to the Italian capital.

There were good reasons for contemplating this move. One was that General Clark, for whom Rome was the "all-consuming interest," as Martin Blumenson puts it, was now concerned about winning because the advantage had been shifted to the Eighth Army. "Moreover," according to the official history, ". . . Clark was very much concerned about reaching Rome before the beginning of Overlord, as General Marshall had frequently and pointedly urged him to do." The history explains further:

"The Alban Hills had become in Clark's eyes a gateway rather than a barrier to Rome. . . . [A]s long as the enemy held the hills in strength a threat remained to the flank of any thrust from the beachhead in the direction of Valmontone and Highway 6. Clark believed that his forces should secure the Alban Hills before attempting to cut off the *Tenth Army's* right wing at Valmontone."

Accordingly, Clark told Truscott to plan for an offensive that could be gotten under way—within 24 hours' notice—along one of four possible axes. The two generals had actually been discussing these plans for some time as alternatives for VI Corps. One thought was to recapture the lost ground around Carroceto and improve present positions to facilitate the eventual capture of Albano or Cisterna. The second was to capture Cisterna, then make a deeper penetration to prepare for operations against Cori or Artena. The third was to capture Littoria, to the east, which would make the beachhead larger; and the last was to capture Ardea, on the western flank, which would not only enlarge the beachhead but threaten the German right flank as well. Truscott's staff had then analyzed the advantages and disadvantages of each plan. According to the VI Corps estimate, attacks to retake Carroceto or to capture Cisterna were the only ones that would be worth the effort.

Four basic plans were formulated during the respite, but when they emerged again after Clark's order for their formal preparation, they had code names and specific axes. Grasshopper was in the direction of Littoria-Sezze; Buffalo was for Cisterna-Cori-Valmontone; Turtle was to take Carroceto-Campoleone-Rome; and Crawdad was to go in the direction of Ardea-Rome. Buffalo was the one that corresponded most closely to Alexander's concept for both Shingle and Diadem, because its objective was to block Highway 6 and cut off the retreat of part of the Tenth Army. Turtle, on the other hand, exactly matched Clark's current thinking concerning the

Traffic-directing MP works from a dugout

mission of VI Corps. Clark later wrote in his memoirs that the difficulty with Buffalo was that "in order to get to Valmontone the beachhead forces would more or less bypass the Alban Hills, leaving the enemy holding high ground that was vital to us if we were to enter Rome." The Fifth Army commander also felt that the Valmontone plan would not in reality trap many Germans, because there were numerous routes the Tenth Army could use to escape to the north.

It was not until 2 April that Alexander formally presented his concept for the use of VI Corps. During the same commanders' conference in which he outlined his plans for the offensive on the southern front, Alexander chose Valmontone as the immediate VI Corps objective, the one that would to his mind accomplish the job of trapping the major part of the Tenth Army. This attack, said Alexander, should be capable of being launched on 24 hours' notice.

General Truscott thought the Valmontone plan would work if it was properly timed with the thrust of the Eighth Army in its advance north through the Liri Valley. When he and General Clark discussed the situation, however, they decided that if the opportunity arose, VI Corps should be prepared to exploit its current position on the flank and to the rear of the Germans. If the Tenth Army were to withdraw too quickly from the south, then an attack toward Carroceto and to the west of the Colli Laziali "might be the quickest way to turn the German position and capture Rome." In any event, Truscott's staff spent the month of April preparing orders and annexes for Grasshopper, Buffalo, Turtle and Crawdad. In the greatest secrecy VI Corps sited artillery, stored ammunition at key locations, selected assembly areas and conducted detailed reconnaissance. One thing that was discovered was that the breakout could not be launched within the 24 hours after notification, because of the need to have the darkness of two nights to move—clandestinely—various units and their supporting weapons to the attack positions. During April, Truscott was left to his own devices while making his breakout preparations, for neither Clark nor Alexander visited VI Corps. Toward the end of the month, Truscott did, however, secure Fifth Army "command post" approval of the four plans.

Then on 5 May Truscott had a visitor, General Alexander. "With some measure of pride," as he said later, he told the AAI commander about the four VI Corps plans and the extent of the preparations made to execute them. Alexander, in turn and with firmness, not only emphasized that Buffalo was the one attack that was worthwhile and the only one that would be launched, but said that he reserved for himself "the decision as to when he proposed to initiate it." Truscott promptly reported the conversation to Clark, who became rather irked at what he felt was interference on the part of Alexander in the "American chain of command." According to Truscott, General Clark, during a visit to Anzio the next day, remarked that "the capture of Rome is the only important objective." Clark was uneasy because he believed that the "British were laying devious plans to be first in Rome." Clark, said Truscott, was determined that the Fifth Army be first instead.

As it turned out, General Clark instructed General Truscott also to be ready to fight in that direction—Plan Turtle. On 7 May, Truscott reported to Fifth Army,

"When present work has been finished, I will be prepared to launch not only Buffalo but either Grasshopper (in case the attack on the southern front bogged down completely) or Turtle within 48 hours. However, if definite preparatory commitment is made to either Grasshopper or Buffalo, and I am then required to launch Turtle, I will need 72 hours in which to make the necessary shift and launch the attack."

Clark in the meantime had informed Alexander that he believed the AAI commander had interfered in his command by issuing instructions to Truscott that were contrary to his own, that is, a firm commitment to one plan as opposed to maintaining flexibility by having several ready to execute. Later on, Clark got the feeling that Alexander, who had said that he had not intended to interfere, believed that the Fifth Army was not "all-out" for the attack. Clark cited his various objections to Buffalo and pointed out that he merely did not want to have to follow any rigid, preconceived ideas in the breakout, and that if the Allies played their cards right they had a chance for a great victory.

144

Troops of the 1st Special Service Force advance toward the hills

On 17 May, as the Fifth and Eighth Armies were making their way north, Clark again broached the question concerning VI Corps. Which way would it attack out of the Anzio beachhead? Alexander remained firm in his conviction that Valmontone was the objective, and that by using fast, mobile patrols the two Allied forces could trap large numbers of Germans between them. Once again General Clark disagreed, arguing only that the I Parachute Corps would be intact on the VI Corps left flank because it would have been untouched in the Alban Hills. He again asked for flexibility:

> "It seems to me, that we should keep ourselves in a position to evaluate the situation when the time comes, and it may prove then that the Cori-Valmontone direction is the wrong one.
>
> We left it that way, with Alexander still feeling that it would be best to cut Route No. 6 at Valmontone in an effort to trap the Germans opposing the Eighth Army."

One day later, Clark called Truscott to the Fifth Army command post to discuss the feasibility of having VI Corps conduct Buffalo as planned, but sending only the Canadian-American 1st Special Service Force on to Valmontone after capturing Cisterna and Cori. At that point, a regrouping would take place and a new attack would be launched northwest out of Cisterna. According to General Truscott, "Clark was obviously still fearful that the British might beat him to Rome."

Meanwhile the FEC and II Corps were getting closer to Terracina and Pico. Alexander on the 20th had decided, without consulting Clark first, on the basis of erroneous information about Eighth Army progress, to execute Buffalo on the night of the 21st. General Clark was shocked that such a decision had been made without his being consulted, and here in his memoirs he finally gives the underlying reasons for his determination to be first in Rome:

> The Fifth Army had had an extremely difficult time throughout the winter campaign and . . . we were now trying to make up for our earlier slow progress. We had massed all of our strength to take Rome. We were keyed up, and in the heat of battle there were almost certain to be clashes of personalities and ideas over this all-out drive. We not only wanted the honor of capturing Rome, but we felt that we more than deserved it; that it would to a certain extent make up for the buffeting and the frustration we had undergone in keeping up the winter pressure against the Germans. My own feeling was that nothing was going to stop us on our push toward the Italian capital. Not only did we intend to become the first army in fifteen centuries to seize Rome from the south, but we intended to see that the people back home knew that it was the Fifth Army that did the job and knew the price that had been paid for it.

As it turned out, it became necessary to postpone the date of the VI Corps attack until 23 May, because the Eighth Army had not advanced as far as Alexander thought and because of a poor weather forecast that, if true, would mean no air support. Clark told Alexander at this point that he was directing II Corps to break through the Hitler Line north of Fondi, "and when it does I am going all out to join up with the bridgehead." Alexander agreed, and it was also planned that the British Eighth would likewise launch its renewed effort on the 23d.

On the German side there was a problem very similar to the one within Allied command relationships: fundamental differences in strategy between Kesselring and Mackensen. Kesselring was convinced that when the Allies broke out of Anzio they would go directly to Valmontone—Buffalo. Mackensen believed that Clark would send his forces to the Alban Hills by way of Highway 7—Turtle. The differences in German thinking were complicated by continuing interference on the part of Hitler concerning tactics in the Italian theater. In what was a compromise with Hitler—not Mackensen—Kesselring ordered certain new defensive positions prepared in key areas like the Factory and Cisterna. Once the Allied attack was identified as the main effort, the forward echelons in these locations would fall back to the newly prepared rear positions, allowing the attackers to move in quickly and expend themselves. Then the elements that had fallen back, together with those on the flanks that had remained forward, would counterattack violently, destroying the incursion. In early April, Kesselring ordered the partial planned evacuation, because it seemed that an attack was imminent, but when by early May none developed, he had the line restored. By this time, Kesselring had come to believe that the Allied thrust would no longer come at Anzio but be made either at the southern front or possibly in the form of another amphibious operation.

During the several weeks of the lull, the Germans had had to shuffle their units to provide both for recuperation and for some strengthening of weak spots along the perimeter. The Hermann Göring Division was withdrawn to Leghorn to rest; the 29th and 26th Panzer Grenadier Divisions were withdrawn from the Fourteenth Army and put in Kesselring's reserves near Rome. Two corps still faced the Allies. I Parachute Corps on the German right commanded the 4th Parachute, 65th Infantry and 3d Panzer Grenadier Divisions; LXXVI Panzer Corps, with its 362d and 715th Infantry Divisions, was on the left. Some replacements had been received during the respite, but Mackensen's forces would never be as strong as they had been in February; his 70,000 men were about 20,000 fewer than the number fielded by the Allies. Mackensen had other problems, too. His artillery units had suffered extensive losses as a result of having been favorite VI Corps targets, and transportation delays had caused shortages in ammunition. Owing to a lack of longer-range artillery, Mackensen was outgunned, but Kesselring had requested 19 batteries of heavy artillery from the German high command. These were en route to Anzio.

At the beachhead, General Truscott had, prior to the attack, seven full divisions. They included the British 1st and 5th Divisions, all of the 1st Armored Division, the American 34th Division (which had relieved the 3d on line during the respite), the 45th Division, the 3d Division and, arriving on 22 May, the 36th Division of Major General Fred L. Walker. Also included in Truscott's formidable attack force was the 1st SSF. On the perimeter from left to right were the British 5th and 1st Divisions, the 45th Division, the 34th Division and the 1st SSF. In his planning, and in spite of General Clark's determination to head directly to Rome, Truscott concentrated on Buffalo, the operation he thought was most likely to be adopted. The VI Corps commander knew that Cisterna, the main German strongpoint, and Cori would both have to be taken quickly. Without these two towns, the enemy would be unable to control the road net leading to Alexander's main objective—Valmontone.

Truscott planned to use as his main assault force the 3d Infantry, the 1st Armored and a reinforced 1st SSF, all of which would attack northeast after having passed through the 34th Division. The 1st Armored would be on the left, the 3d Division in the middle and the 1st SSF on the right. General Harmon's tankers were to capture Valmontone, while the 3d Division was given the task of taking the long-elusive Cisterna, a job that General O'Daniel approached with pleasure. On the left flank of the main attack, the 45th Division was to advance past Carano. Meanwhile, on the left of the VI Corps the two British divisions were to deceive the enemy with

Valmontone—the object of Operation Buffalo

local attacks. The plan called for the British divisions to be detached from VI Corps on 22 May and come under the control of the Fifth Army. After the main attack was launched, the 36th Division was to move up to take Cori and reinforce the 1st Armored at Artena, a town on the way to Valmontone. Major General Charles W. Ryder's 34th Division was to be prepared to relieve elements in the main attack whenever called upon to do so.

    As had been the case so often before, the breakout was to be assisted by a massive artillery preparation, this one against targets that had been carefully located and selected during the respite. Allied aircraft from MAAF were to help as well, with targets in the Alban Hills, Velletri and Valmontone being bombed and strafed daily prior to the breakout attempt.

    Postponement of the offensive until 23 May created an unforeseen danger to VI Corps, because the units that had clandestinely been moved into their attack positions were now required to remain longer than intended, thus increasing the possibility that the Germans would detect what was going on. On the 21st, Truscott received official orders to begin Buffalo at 0630 on the 23d, and by daylight of the 22d the infantrymen were in their forward assembly areas, ready to go.

General Clark, who had arrived at his advance command post on 22 May, awaited the start of the offensive, confident of the outcome. He was worried, however, about the political problems surrounding this aspect of the Italian campaign. Although he had ordered the attack to begin as Alexander wished, he had ensured that VI Corps could switch the direction of advance to the Colli Laziali—and Rome. According to the official history, Clark thought by this time that adhering to Alexander's plan "was pointless." Clark himself said, "I was determined that the Fifth Army was going to capture Rome and I probably was overly sensitive to indications that practically everybody else was trying to get into the act."

On the night before the breakout was to begin, the two British divisions on the VI Corps left flank began their diversionary attacks as planned, two brigades strong. General Truscott, who was there when it happened, provided this description of the beginning of the attack.

0545! There was a crash of thunder and bright lightning flashes against the sky behind us as more than a thousand guns, infantry cannon, mortars, tanks and tank destroyers opened fire. That first crash settled into a continuous rumbling roar. Some distance ahead, a wall of fire appeared as our first salvos crashed into the enemy front lines, then tracers wove eerie patterns in streaks of light as hundreds of machine guns of every caliber poured a hail of steel into the enemy positions. Where we stood watching, the ground quivered and trembled. Day was now breaking, but a pall of smoke and dust shrouded the battle area. At the end of forty minutes, the guns fell silent. Then, from the southeast, appeared three groups of fighters and light bombers, their silvery wings glinting in the morning light. Towering clouds of smoke and dust broke through the pall about Cisterna as their bombs crashed into the town and enemy positions. Five minutes, and the planes were gone. The artillery began anew. H hour had come and the battle was on.

Although there was a slight drizzle as the attack got under way at 0630, the day remained hazy from smokescreens and the dust and smoke of battle. This condition helped the Americans in their move northeast, because German observers were unable accurately to direct the fire of their artillery batteries. All along the front, from Carano to the Mussolini Canal, American tanks and infantrymen emerged from inside the smoke and haze. The attempt at a breakout was now a reality.

Truscott had assigned General Harmon's armored troops the specific task of advancing west of Cisterna along the left flank of the 3d Division. This was fairly open terrain, and the ground had dried sufficiently to permit the use of armor off the roads. Harmon attacked in his sector with two combat commands (CCs) abreast, CCA to the left and CCB to the right.

Observation plane lands behind smoke screen

One major problem facing the Americans was that the enemy, anything but inactive during the weeks of quiet, had sown extensive minefields all along the front, creating a threat more dangerous to the tankers than antitank weapons. The decision as to how to defeat the minefields was left to the combat command commanders. One opted for mine detectors operated by the engineers, the other decided to use explosive snakes. Thus engineer troops had to work all night long to clear the mines for the armored units they supported. For the tankers that had chosen to rely on snakes, the explosives were detonated as the armored vehicles crossed the LD after having passed through the 34th Division.

The GIs of the 1st Armored Division found the fighting extremely rough during the first day as they slowly made their way through the mines to their first objective, a low ridge north of the railway between Cisterna and Campoleone. In spite of the care taken to overcome the minefields, casualties were heavy; even an uncharted American minefield took its toll. By nightfall, however, Harmon's men had punctured the German main line of resistance, reached their objective and begun to consolidate their positions. For the German defenders, the armored advance represented a serious incursion into their lines. It had penetrated more than a mile almost at the boundary between the I Parachute and LXXVI Panzer Corps, against understrength units of the 362d Division.

General O'Daniel's 3d Division did not fare as well. Cisterna, the key objective for all of Buffalo because it controlled the roads leading to Velletri, Cori and Valmontone, was still firmly in the hands of the Germans at the close of the day. The 3d Division infantrymen faced a regiment of the German 362d Division and the right half of the 715th Division, which had been reinforced by another regiment—such was the importance the enemy placed on the retention of Cisterna. Plans for the 3d Division called for the use of all three regiments, the 7th to be used in a frontal attack while the other two, the 30th and the 15th, enveloped the town from the left and the right. After the division began its attack, it soon became evident that mines, as well as a determined enemy resistance, would be as troublesome in this sector as they had been in General Harmon's area, at least for two of the three regiments. The German defenders put up a stiff battle all along the line, refusing to give more than a few yards at a time.

Along the route of advance of a unit of the 15th Regiment—Company E of the 2d Battalion—an attack against a strong enemy force concealed in a wooded area came to an unusual climax. According to the official history:

"With ammunition running short and anxious to take advantage of the supporting tank fire's keeping the enemy under cover, Company E's commander ordered his men to fix bayonets and charge. In one of the few verified bayonet assaults by American troops during World War II, the men dashed into the woods and swarmed over the German positions. They killed 15 of the enemy and captured 80, while an undetermined number broke from the far side of the woods and fled."

Although the 3d Division had not gained nearly the ground by the end of the day that had been taken by the 1st Armored Division, it suffered 1,626 casualties, compared with 173 for the tankers. The two enemy divisions, which had been well dug in all along the 3d Division's attack route, responded to each American move with a hail of small arms fire, which—together with the minefields—kept the division's gains for the day to only half the distance from the LD to Cisterna.

General Eagles's 45th Division, in its limited attack to the left of the 1st Armored Division, required two of its regiments to attack along a northerly axis to the northwest of Carano. For the 45th, mines presented few problems, and the advances were relatively quick. In one instance, the 180th Regiment overran an entire German battalion and captured its commander while he was still in his CP. On the other hand, in a strong counterattack to Eagles's quick penetration of the enemy MLR, somewhere between 15 and 24 Tiger tanks tore through the ranks of a battalion of the 157th Regiment. Before General Truscott could counterattack with tanks and infantry from the 1st Armored Division's reserves, Allied artillery was called into play. A furious barrage, including fire from 8-inch howitzers, was unleashed, completely routing the German tanks. They fled, leaving several of their vehicles behind and the 45th Division in possession of the objectives for the day.

On the extreme right of the VI Corps assault was General Frederick's 1st SSF, which by noon had pushed across Highway 7 and almost to the railroad running southeast out of Cisterna. Frederick was holding his men back to allow the 15th Regiment of the 3d Division to catch up, when the Germans counterattacked with tanks and infantry in a force large enough to threaten penetration of the SSF's forward ranks. Responding to the G-3's declaration that "all hell has broken loose up here," VI Corps sent reinforcements. Nevertheless, part of one company was cut off, and the lead regiment had to fall back behind the highway. Lacking reserves, the Germans were unable to exploit their gains, and after a brief period of reorganization General Frederick's men were able to recover the ground they had lost. Because of the fury of this fight and the severity of the casualty figure in the lead regiment, General Truscott replaced it with a battalion from the 34th Division.

Kesselring and Mackensen had no question, by dusk on the 23d, that the Allies had unleashed their long-planned breakout attempt. Despite the German stand in front of Cisterna, the Fourteenth Army's situation map looked grim. Because both the 362d and 715th Divisions had taken such a beating, the Hermann Göring Division was being rushed back into the battle from Leghorn. Mackensen requested permission from Kesselring to

Park in the Cisterna town square—remains of a German strongpoint

Men wounded at Cisterna help each other to a hospital area

withdraw the part of the 715th Division that was south of Cisterna to the railway line. But OB SÜD ordered the Fourteenth Army to stand fast and stabilize the lines with LXXVI Corps reserves. Kesselring feared that if he allowed the corps left flank to be pulled back, the move would cause a vacuum between the Tenth and Fourteenth Armies, north of Terracina, that could quickly be exploited by the Allies.

Since Kesselring was sure that the attack by the two British divisions was diversionary and that the Allies had already revealed in the attempt to take Cisterna the direction of their main thrust, he suggested also that certain I Parachute Corps units be shifted to the LXXVI Corps front lines. Mackensen, however, was still fearful that Clark would try to take Rome by way of Highway 7, and was unwilling to weaken I Parachute Corps for this reason. The Fourteenth Army moved available antitank guns to LXXVI Corps, but little else. Also, in keeping with the original thinking concerning German strategy around Anzio, Mackensen required I Corps to withdraw to secondary defensive positions. LXXVI Corps, meanwhile, planned to stiffen its defenses as best it could from units on its extreme left flank.

General Truscott thought that the first day of the breakout attempt had gone well. American losses had been heavy, but the damage to the enemy had been greater, as evidenced by the 1,500 German prisoners on hand at the end of the day. Fighter-bombers were active over the entire battlefield as Buffalo moved into its second day—24 May, just two weeks before the Normandy invasion. For the 1st Armored Division, the order of the day was to continue the drive to the northeast. Both its combat commands were to cross Highway 7 and occupy a phase line about 2,000 yards northeast of the railroad, after which CCA would veer north to Velletri and CCB would turn toward a small village, Giulianello, which was halfway between Cori and Velletri.

By nightfall, after a slow and hard-fought advance, parts of the phase line had been occupied, and even passed by. CCB had succeeded in gaining ground to a point due north of Cisterna, in effect accomplishing a partial envelopment of the village. CCA, to the left of its counterpart, was able to advance quickly against what was in reality a German fighting withdrawal, to a point only four miles from Velletri.

Cisterna was still the main target for the 3d Division, which very nearly succeeded in capturing the town. Continuing with the 30th Infantry on the left, the 7th in the middle and the 15th on the right, the attack was pressed with determination. Again the enemy put up a strong stand, and again O'Daniel's infantry made limited but significant advances. By late afternoon the 7th Regiment was across Highway 7 and occupying the cemetery at Cisterna. The 30th Infantry, in a confusing maneuver that actually saw it cross the rear echelons of the 7th Infantry as the latter was making an attack on Cisterna, reached a point northeast of the town early on the 25th. It was actually not far from the tankers of Combat Command B. The 15th Regiment met stiff enemy resistance, especially at the railroad, in its attempt to envelop the village from the right, but by dark it had crossed the tracks and advanced some 500 yards beyond. Late that evening, in the attack that saw the confusion between the two regiments, the 7th Infantry tried once again to take Cisterna, but failed.

While the 1st Armored and 3d Infantry Divisions were making their way forward on the 24th, the 45th Division was holding fast to its positions northwest of Carano. At sundown, however, the enemy mounted a strong counterattack with both infantry and tanks. Not until the Germans were within 100 yards of the division lines were they discovered, and a battle that included hand-to-hand fighting promptly ensued. The regiment that was hit—the 180th—had its lines pushed back slightly, but by midnight the front was restored, as the enemy withdrew. Action for the 1st SSF was limited on the 24th to preparations for a thrust the next day to Monte Arrestino, about two miles south of Cori.

On 24 May, General von Mackensen finally secured from Field Marshal Kesselring permission to withdraw part of the 715th Division. But Mackensen went on to exceed the authority given him and ordered the entire unit to fall back to a line from Cisterna to the Lepini Mountains. Late

Troops of the U.S. 7th Regiment line up Germans at Cisterna

in the day the 362d Division, whose commander had just returned from emergency leave in Germany, took stock of the grim situation. The division then requested approval to withdraw its garrison at Cisterna. Kesselring refused, but Mackensen once more disobeyed orders and instructed the 362d to go ahead with the pullout. By the time the division commander was notified, however, it was too late—contact could not be made with the beleaguered garrison, which had entrenched itself deep in the city. To make matters worse, no reinforcements were yet available for the Fourteenth Army. Not only had the Hermann Göring Division not arrived from Leghorn, but Mackensen still declined to use units from his right flank to strengthen LXXVI Corps defenses in the Cisterna sector. Adding further to the Germans' difficulties on the 24th, relations between Kesselring and Mackensen had become so strained as to be almost at the breaking point.

For the 25th, General Truscott planned simply to capitalize on the gains made during the first two days of the breakout attempt. Because the two combat commands of the 1st Armored Division were now advancing on diverging axes, Truscott ordered the 34th Division to take control, behind the armor, of a five-mile stretch of the line north of Cisterna. At the same time, VI Corps ordered the reserve 36th Division engineers to constitute a force to move south to contact Fifth Army's II Corps as it came north out of Terracina. The linkup between the two corps occurred during the morning, and for the first time in the long fight in Italy, Anzio was no longer a beachhead. It was now the left flank of the Fifth Army.

Harmon's CCA continued to try to advance toward Velletri on the 25th, but the pressure exerted by the Germans became much more intense. The Americans lost a number of tanks during an enemy counterattack, and were held to their advances of the previous day. CCB, meanwhile, made preparations to accompany and support the 15th Infantry in an advance upon Cori.

To add to the pressure against the Germans, General Harmon had constituted a strong armor-infantry task force—Task Force Howze—that on the 25th pushed out quickly, cut the highway between Cori and Velletri and captured the village of Giulianello. This move was decisive. It bisected the German line at the boundary between the 715th and 362d Divisions, caused the surrender of a large number of enemy soldiers and threatened with an envelopment the part of the 715th still south of the Lepini Mountains. Although, on the 25th, a regiment from another Fourteenth Army division was finally ordered to reinforce the 715th near Cori, it arrived too late to provide any sort of assistance.

After a slow start, infantrymen of the 15th Regiment attacked toward Cori at midmorning, and by dusk the Americans actually had patrols in the village, which seemed to be devoid of Germans. As for Cisterna, the 7th Infantry launched its attack to capture the village. The outlying portions were quickly taken, but in the center of town it was a different matter. What was left of the 362d Division's garrison had holed up in a do-or-die effort to keep Cisterna in German hands. For almost the entire day, in spite of the fact that they were in effect under siege, the Germans stood fast behind well-prepared defenses. Finally, late in the afternoon, the resistance weakened, and American infantrymen at last occupied what was the preeminent objective of the Anzio campaign.

With the fall of Cisterna, and with Cori all but in Allied hands, the second phase of Buffalo had been completed. Valmontone lay only a few miles to the north. Tactically, all appeared to be going well. But the plan was due to be changed—not an entirely unexpected move at VI Corps. On 24 May, General Clark had asked General Truscott whether he had considered changing the direction of the VI Corps advance toward Rome instead of Valmontone. Truscott replied that he had, but that such a move could only be worthwhile if the forces of I Parachute Corps were moved from the Colli Laziali to the Valmontone area. If they were, it might cause VI Corps to be delayed at Valmontone "long enough to permit the German main forces to escape . . . [in which case] an attack to the northwest might be the best way to cut off the enemy withdrawal north of the Alban Hills."

Truscott had kept Turtle current on a day-to-day basis, but this was the first time—since discussions before the breakout attempt was launched—that he had been reminded of General Clark's wishes to change Buffalo to Turtle. According to the official history, "Truscott was puzzled over Clark's apparent desire to tinker with an operation that seemed to be moving rapidly to a successful conclusion." Clark, however, continued in his belief that Alexander's strategy was not correct, and as the VI Corps breakout progressed and more information on German movements became available, he became "more and more convinced that instead of continuing a major effort toward Valmontone and Highway 6, he should be driving straight for Rome."

Intelligence received by the Fifth Army served to strengthen Clark's thesis: the Germans were building up their strength near Valmontone. The 362d Division had withdrawn to that area, the Hermann Göring Division had been ordered into the "Valmontone Gap," and there was a chance that Mackensen would shift some I Parachute Corps units toward the town. Clark concluded that two factors were militating against continuing the attack as desired by Alexander. The first was the apparent buildup of forces in Valmontone; the second was the fact that the American front, which extended from Anzio almost to the town, was becoming increasingly vulnerable to German attack from the north.

> "Without further staff discussion on the subject," observes the official history, "Clark decided to modify Operation Buffalo significantly and turn the bulk of Truscott's corps northwestward into the Alban Hills.
>
> On 25 May Clark directed his G-3 . . . to inform General Truscott of the new objective."

That objective was Rome.

New bridge replaces stone structure destroyed by shelling

12. Rome

Dawn on May 25 found the German forces in a desperate situation along Highway 6. Convoys, hurrying to escape from the Liri Valley, were pouring northwest by day and night. Allied fighters and bombers punished the moving columns at will, claiming 645 vehicles destroyed and 446 damaged for the day's total. According to Eric Linklater, there was a "fantastic litter of blackened, twisted wrecks, of tanks and lorries and troop carriers and guns and command cars, that remained on the roads from Cori to Giulianello, from Velletri to Valmontone."

Below Velletri the 1st Armored Division was poised to exploit the collapse of German resistance south of Highway 6. The 3d Division had all but captured Cori, and the 1st SSF was taking the mountains overlooking the highway. Considering the state of things in that area, General Truscott had great expectations: "By the following morning, we would be astride the German line of withdrawal through Valmontone." The right flank of the German Tenth Army would, in effect, be caught in a pocket between the advancing Allied armies and the Simbruini Mountains, a range to the east of Rome. All in all, Truscott was well pleased with the progress and prospects of VI Corps.

On returning to his command post at noon after visits to the field,

Truscott found Brigadier General Donald Brann, General Clark's G-3, waiting to see him. Brann had orders from Clark for VI Corps to implement Turtle, but to leave the 3d Division and 1st SSF to cut Route 6 and take Valmontone. Truscott was "dumbfounded." Protesting that "conditions were not right," he later wrote, he argued that "this was not time to drive to the northwest where the enemy was still strong." Thoroughly convinced that the main thrust should still be toward Highway 6, Truscott felt he could not comply with the order until he had talked personally with Clark. Brann informed Truscott that the Fifth Army commander could not be reached and that the order had to be carried out. Only then did Truscott implement it. His judgment after the war was that this order "turned the main effort of the beachhead forces from the Valmontone Gap and prevented the destruction of the German Tenth Army."

When informed of the new orders, division commanders were hesitant. That day had seen the fall of Cisterna and Giulianello, and VI Corps was on the verge of accomplishing its original mission as specified in Buffalo. Generals O'Daniel and Harmon were especially disturbed because this change meant a weakening of forces on their front at a particularly crucial time. The plan, as Truscott described it to them,

> "was to concentrate the 34th Infantry Division southwest of Velletri, and then move northwest with the 34th and 45th Infantry Divisions abreast to sieze the line Lanuvio-Campoleone. While this was under way, we could relieve the 1st Armored Division with the 36th Infantry Division opposite Velletri, then move the 1st Armored Division across the rear of the 34th and 45th Infantry Divisions to the Carano-Padiglione area in readiness to join with the 45th Infantry Division in the drive on Campoleone. Meanwhile, the 3d Infantry Division, with the 1st Special Service Force and Task Force Howze attached, would block Highway 6 in the vicinity of Valmontone."

This plan necessitated appalling shifts in troops, relocations of command posts and displacements of artillery. Complicated routing of traffic over limited road nets could be accomplished, according to Truscott, "only because staff preparation was thorough and complete and . . . carried out by well-trained and disciplined troops; and because enemy capabilities for interference were limited."

Within 12 hours, or literally overnight, the 45th and 34th Divisions swung the attack toward Campoleone station and Lanuvio, respectively. Intelligence reported only a "hodgepodge" of German units along this front and said that breakthrough could be attained by concentrating the two divisions on this relatively narrow three-mile sector. According to the VI Corps G-2, I Parachute Corps manned the German line from the Alban Hills to the Tyrrhenian Sea and had now weakened its defenses by shifting units to help at Cisterna and Valmontone. This estimate, though called "reasonably accurate," was misleading, because I Parachute Corps was still very strong and mostly intact. General von Mackensen, who had always believed that VI Corps's main thrust would come west of the Alban Hills, had refused to move more than a few units from I Parachute Corps toward the threat against LXXXVI Panzer Corps. As at the Anzio landing, the enemy drew on various units from behind the front, gambling on his ability to move to a critical area at the right time. The term "hodgepodge" more properly applied to the Valmontone area than to I Parachute Corps's front.

The new offensive started well on the morning of 26 May, but German resistance increased and casualties mounted during the next two days. Kesselring, at last realizing the precariousness of the Tenth Army's position, abandoned plans for its reinforcement and concentrated instead on saving as much of it as possible. Throwing everything he could into the Valmontone area—a rocket launcher unit from the 334th Division, an infantry regiment and an antiaircraft battery—he sought to hold the Allied forces long enough to bring forward the Hermann Göring Division.

Forty miles to the southeast the British Eighth Army was advancing up the Liri Valley, pushing back the covering forces of the Tenth Army. Between the fronts of the two Allied armies were the retreating German forces, which afforded tantalizing targets for the MAAF and were potential prey for the 1st SSF and 3d Infantry Division. At first little opposition was encountered by the Allies. Progress on the 26th was so rapid that American fighter-bombers mistook the Allied forward columns for enemy troops and attacked them. Cori, now in American hands, was also accidentally bombed, which complicated the movement of troops through the town and beyond in pursuit of the enemy. At Rocca Massima an entire German infantry regiment was surprised and captured. Colonel Hamilton Howze's task force forged ahead on the 3d Division's left flank, coming within 800 yards of Highway 6, two miles northwest of Valmontone, to be halted there by antitank fire. General O'Daniel was elated by this rapid progress and so reported to Truscott: "This area is very soft . . . I'm convinced we could go on to Rome, if we had more stuff up here." But evidence that elements of the Hermann Göring Division (just arriving from Leghorn) were present convinced O'Daniel that Howze's armor could be in danger; it therefore was withdrawn from near Highway 6 to the main body of the task force, which was then west of Artena.

Unaware of the rapid advance of the 3d Division, Kesselring withheld reinforcement of the reconnaissance units of the Hermann Göring Division by the main body. This division had had a difficult time and was arriving, in some instances, without its heavy equipment. Realizing the imminent danger, the division commander, General Wilhelm Schmalz, gave orders of his own to reverse the situation. When Kesselring angrily rebuked him and ordered the Hermann Göring Division troops withdrawn, Schmalz ignored him. Kesselring, with more information, later endorsed Schmalz's move and an effective block was thrown against the surging Fifth Army.

By the next day, 27 May, the enemy was strong enough to mount counterattacks near Artena and hold the 3d Division there, on the defensive. The German counterattack of the 27th seemed suicidal to the Americans, as it came across open fields in broad daylight. Outposts of Howze's task force, still to the left of the 3d Division, asked whether the troops might be Americans, to which Colonel Howze answered, "Hell no, shoot them up!" Racing to the front line, Howze found that the Germans had approached within 1,500 yards before the American tank guns had opened fire, decimating the enemy ranks.

The remainder of the Hermann Göring Division attacked at 1930, using self-propelled guns to destroy two American tanks. Artillery fire, German and Allied short rounds alike, sent task-force infantrymen to cover. A group of 160 replacements arrived just as the artillery opened up. Half of them were killed or wounded. Attempting to stop the short rounds, three American artillery observers and an infantry battalion commander were killed by flying shell fragments as they were radioing the fire-control section. Withdrawing about 1,500 yards, Colonel Howze finally left the German counterattack to the mercy of the artillery. Firing round after round, British and American batteries so devastated the enemy that Howze was able to move his men back to their abandoned positions early the next day.

Colonel Howze's task force was relieved on the 28th by the 7th Infantry, 3d Division. Part of the task force reverted to its parent unit, the 1st Armored Division, which was on its way to the front at Campoleone to join the 45th Division. The rest of the task force was temporarily put in reserve. On the VI Corps right flank the 1st SSF had meanwhile surged beyond Monte Arrestino.

General Keyes's II Corps, having made contact with VI Corps on 25 May south of Anzio, was now so positioned as to give General Clark strong new forces with which to renew the attack on Valmontone. On 30 May, General Keyes relinquished the II Corps zone to the newly formed IV Corps and moved his headquarters to the Artena sector. There II Corps, in addition to its own 85th and 88th Divisions from the southern front, took command of the 3d Division, Howze's Task Force and the 1st SSF.

In the Lepini Mountains the French Expeditionary Corps was ideally placed for a drive on Ferrentino, which was officially in the British zone of responsibility. A Fifth Army request for permission to move into this part of the British zone precipitated a stiff argument. General Alexander, who had received word of Clark's swing to the northwest 15 minutes after it had begun, was disinclined. He would agree to the move only if the FEC would step aside for the Eighth Army when it arrived. The British, still several days to the southeast, could not otherwise be brought into the battle for Rome. But Alexander promised that if the Fifth Army took Valmontone, Clark would be authorized to use Route 6 for an attack on Rome.

GIs move through rubble that was once Valmontone

The Eighth Army would later pass through Valmontone but bypass Rome.

General Juin, sensing that his valiant FEC would be left behind, was keenly disappointed. General Clark wrote later, "The immediate result [was] that the French Expeditionary Corps, which actually had sparked the whole drive toward Rome, was being squeezed out of our front and more or less left dangling in the mountains south of the Liri." Clark and Juin, deciding "that the attack would not work under such conditions," left Ferrentino to the British. The FEC would instead push through the mountains toward Valmontone; it would form the right flank of the Fifth Army. General Clark's admiration for the FEC led him to say "a more gallant fighting organization never existed," and he promised Juin "that from there [Valmontone] on I would, by hook or crook, arrange to have his forces assist in the II Corps attack on Rome."

The night of 27 May found VI Corps's 45th and the 34th Divisions two miles southeast of their objectives, Campoleone and Lanuvio. After two days of fighting on this supposedly weak front, the expected breakthrough still eluded the Allies. On the next day the 1st Armored Division began to assemble behind the 45th for the planned attack with General Eagles's Division. The attack commenced on the 29th with CCB on the left, CCA on the right and the infantrymen of the 45th following. Resistance at first was light, but it increased as the armor approached the Caesar Line, another German defense. In their exuberance, Harmon's tanks forged ahead too quickly, leaving enemy strongpoints behind to hold up the infantrymen. This temporarily disrupted the cooperation and coordination between armor and infantry that had been carefully planned for this particular phase of the offensive.

In response to the appearance of American armored units in the Campoleone area, Mackensen requested reinforcements, and on his own began collecting whatever antitank weapons he could find. Kesselring had little to offer except the antiaircraft artillery from OB SÜD reserves, amounting to 14 batteries. Supplementing this force, I Corps laid new minefields in an attempt to halt or at least slow the American thrust. Mackensen was counting strongly on the Caesar Line to hold the Fifth Army long enough to withdraw beyond Rome. The capital would then become a screen for his army.

South of Lanuvio in the 34th Division sector, two particularly formidable German strongpoints, San Gennaro Hill and the Villa Crocetta, faced the Americans. Mortars and machine guns covered the open fields below, and obstacles and barbed wire protected the approaches. A division attack on the 29th produced severe fighting. Some gains were made but were soon lost. At one point San Gennaro Hill was taken, but counterattacks drove the 2d Battalion, 168th Infantry, off again. Once more the battalion drove forward, through vicious enemy fire, to take the crest of the hill. Enemy mortars opened fire on its exposed positions, and once more the GIs were forced to withdraw, this time fighting their way through infiltrating enemy forces. Not until after dark did the Americans make their way back to the previous night's line.

To the west, the 1st Battalion, 168th Regiment, had even less success. Infantrymen, crawling through the open grain fields, reached a ravine only a few hundred yards from Villa Crocetta, but were pinned there by enemy machine gun and mortar fire. It was necessary to bring up tanks and tank destroyers to cover their withdrawal. Companies A and C were then ordered to make a frontal assault on the house as soon as Company B with its tanks made an enveloping movement and appeared behind it. Company B's maneuver, however, was so successful that it was able to overrun the villa, driving the enemy troops out. Companies A and C, which could not see the tanks of Company B, remained in position. Meanwhile the Germans, knowing that possession of Villa Crocetta protected the boundary between the 3d Panzer Grenadier and the 362d Infantry Divisions, counterattacked and took a hill overlooking the rear of Company B. The Americans were then forced to return to the original line of departure, and to add insult to injury, one battalion was harassed by 16 rounds of 280-mm fire before retiring.

On 30 May the story was the same for the 34th and 45th and 1st Armored Divisions. During the 1st Armored Division's drive to Campoleone, reinforcements assigned to it had to battle strengthened German positions just to join the units they were reinforcing. General Harmon attacked again with his now-augmented force, but antitank guns and enemy infantrymen with Panzerfausts (rocket launchers) took a high toll—23 tanks destroyed and several others damaged. Casualties were even higher than on the

Advancing infantrymen pass a knocked-out U.S. M4 tank

previous day. The American gain was one mile. The 34th Division also was unable to move successfully to Lanuvio; enemy resistance was too stiff. The official history states that "the only gains made on the 30th were by the British as they crossed the Moletta River on the far left flank." These gains were due mainly to German withdrawals.

As Mackensen and the German Fourteenth Army held the front door to Rome closed on the 45th, 34th and 1st Armored Divisions, the 36th Infantry Division found the back door unlocked. On the night of 27 May, reconnaissance patrols found that Monte Artemisio, a four-mile-long ridge north of Velletri, was undefended. This gap in fact resulted from the severe losses incurred by the 362d Division during the defense of Cisterna and the moving of part of the Hermann Göring Division to the southwest. Hurried attempts to throw the weakened and weary 715th Division and two battalions of the Hermann Göring Division into the breach came too late. Kesselring, on being informed of the gap, ordered Mackensen to close it. Mackensen did nothing more than he had done; he was confident that the 715th and the battalions of the Hermann Göring Division would arrive in time to hold the Allies at the breach. He then turned his attention to the Lariano-Valmontone sector of the line, where things were beginning to happen.

General Walker, 36th Division commander, informed General Truscott of the gap on May 28th and proceeded with plans for the envelopment of Velletri and a dash northward into the Alban Hills. Success would depend on close armor and artillery support. This, in turn, depended on the ability of the engineers to make footpaths and cart trails into passable roads. Communications would have to be maintained over an eight-mile-deep penetration in difficult terrain.

164

Near midnight on the 30th the move was on. The 142d Infantry reached the base of Monte Artemisio by 0130. Just as dawn was breaking, the infantrymen could see before them their objective, the summit of the mountain. By 0630 they were on the top, having surprised the only Germans there—three artillery observers, one still in his morning bath. Not before that afternoon did enemy soldiers along Highway 7 spot the American forces. Walker's men then pressed on to a ridge that overlooked Velletri. By the morning of 1 June, Velletri was virtually surrounded; only Highway 7 remained as an escape route.

Battering an entrenched engineer platoon with an artillery barrage, the 143d Infantry captured another spur, called Maschio d'Ariano. Morning light revealed a 200-degree panorama from the east to the southwest. According to the official history, below the mountain "lay supply arteries of much of the Fourteenth Army, especially those supporting the Lariano-Valmontone sector. Scores of tempting enemy targets crawled across the landscape beneath them." Artillery batteries were alerted and observers brought up to direct the firing. "Soon forward observers were sitting around on the Maschio d'Ariano like crows on a telephone line, having a field day."

On 31 May the Fourteenth Army finally became aware of the penetration. Kesselring was informed late the same day. Mackensen had ordered an immediate counterattack, but this move did not alleviate the fury of his superior. The German response was too late to be effective. Allied artillery attacks on LXXVI Corps communication and supply lines above Valmontone doomed the German stand there to sure defeat. With II Corps poised along Highway 6 and the fall of the city imminent, General Alexander kept his promise and adjusted the Fifth and Eighth Army zones of responsibility so that Clark would be able to use Highway 6 and deploy his three corps across the entire front north of Valmontone and into the hills to the east.

The advance of Walker's 36th Division was the only bright spot in the VI Corps picture as May changed to June. In a morning attack up the Albano road, the 179th Infantry, 45th Division, met such fierce opposition that by midday one company had just one officer and 35 men remaining. Other companies suffered almost as severely. General Eagles was forced to withdraw the regiment and replace it with the 180th Infantry. The afternoon went no better for the division. Ryder's 34th Division meanwhile suffered a repetition of previous engagements, and that evening San Gennaro Ridge and Villa Crocetta were still in German hands. The 36th Division's capture of the high ground above Velletri forced the 362d Infantry Division to withdraw during that night toward Lake Albano, by way of Highway 7.

Kesselring's concern for the elements of the Tenth Army still retreating from the Liri Valley prevented him from allowing Mackensen to draw back farther. Consequently VI Corps suffered another frustrating and costly day on 2 June. General Clark's disappointment at VI Corps's lack of progress was made worse by the fast-approaching date for Overlord, the Normandy invasion. If Rome fell to the Fifth Army after 6 June, the victory would hardly make a ripple in the ocean of public interest, because the world's attention would be on the long-awaited Allied attack on Fortress Europe. Another worry was the possibility of German reinforcements arriving, causing the Fifth Army to have to wait for the British Eighth Army to join it in forcing a breakthrough.

But 2 June brought a change in fortune for the Fifth Army as a whole. Elements of the 36th Division surged forward, threatening the I Parachute Corps's left flank at Nemi and forcing Kesselring to order Mackensen to pull back the entire Fourteenth Army front, except close to the coast where the British divisions were following up the German retreat. All transportation was to be pressed into service—including that necessary for the supply of the civilian population in Rome—in order to bring available reinforcements forward. Under cover of an artillery barrage, the Germans withdrew in the darkness of the night. Dawn on 3 June found Lanuvio in 34th Division hands. The 1st Armored Division, having been brought forward along Highway 7 to a point below Albano, was poised, the 45th Division on the left and the 36th Division in the Alban Hills on the right, for the dash to Rome.

II Corps, now threatening Valmontone, had not been idle. Reinforced by the arrival of the 85th Infantry Division, the Allied forces in the Lariano-Valmontone–Colle Ferro area renewed their offensive on 1 June. Fighting was heavy, as the 85th and 3d Divisions met enemy forces trying to restore contact between the two corps of the Fourteenth Army. On the

The outskirts of Rome: Generals Keyes, Donald Brann, Clark and Frederick study situation maps

far right, however, the 1st SSF took Colle Ferro, cutting Highway 6 and capturing more than 200 Germans. Since these prisoners had formed a large part of the enemy rear guard, their elimination from the fighting guaranteed the FEC, which was south of Colle Ferro, quick passage up Highway 6. At Valmontone heavy motor traffic was heard by Allied outposts. When this was reported to the 3d Division CP, General O'Daniel's comment was heated. "Why don't you put mortar fire on it?" he asked. "Get an AT gun up there and plaster hell out of everything that comes along. You can block the road any place you want to. The important thing is to shoot every goddam vehicle that comes by there."

Valmontone was now untenable. Kesselring therefore gave orders for the Tenth Army's 90th Panzer Grenadier Division to move to Palestrina, where it would be joined by the entire XIV Corps. In Kesselring's mind, if II Corps should turn toward Rome as he was sure it would, a strong force near Palestrina would be in position to harass its flank. This high ground, in the meantime, would have to be held by the left wing of Mackensen's Fourteenth Army, which by this time consisted of only one infantry battalion, four tanks and a diverse collection of artillery.

Morning on 2 June found Valmontone virtually undefended; it had fallen to the 3d Division by 1030. The 88th Division, together with the 85th, made steady headway against covering enemy forces. Above Valmontone the 3d Division had crossed Highway 6 and was pursuing the enemy to the high ground south of Palestrina.

By evening Kesselring realized that his plan for Palestrina would never be possible unless XIV Panzer Corps could counterattack the Fifth Army thrust up Highway 6. Vietinghoff, however, did not possess the strength needed to mount such an attack and ordered his Tenth Army to retreat to the east of Rome. According to the official history, "the Tenth Army's retreat through the [Simbruini] mountains was well conceived and skillfully executed, amply fulfilling Clark's earlier prediction that there were just too many escape routes open to the Germans."

On 3 June II Corps was beyond Valmontone, harassing the withdrawing German troops and probing the hills in what had been, until the previous day, the Eighth Army zone. Only a rapidly retreating enemy was between the corps and Rome.

Rome's singular position in the religious and cultural worlds dictated to both belligerents that an attempt be made to preserve it and its treasures. German orders issued as early as March directed Fourteenth Army soldiers to remain outside the city. Convoys were rerouted and Vatican City was declared off limits. As Allied troops approached on 3 June, Kesselring made an effort, through the Vatican, to have Rome declared an open city. The Allies made their usual reply: AAI in a letter stated that if the Germans chose to fight there, the Allies would "take appropriate measures to eject them." In addition AAI made what some considered to be an irresponsible call for the civilian population to rise against the Germans. Had the Romans responded, vicious street fighting would have ensued. General Clark echoed the rejection of an open-city declaration, stating that "the deciding factor would be the enemy's dispositions and actions." These statements were, all in all, small consolation to the Romans.

Surging forward on 4 June, the 85th Division moved across the northeastern flank of the Alban Hills and down into Frascati, Kesselring's former headquarters. The strongest resistance of the day was from 38 German soldiers from a cooks' and bakers' school near Rome. The 88th Division, augmented by Howze's task force, also moved out, but soon the infantry lagged behind. When antitank guns opened fire, the armor was forced to wait until infantrymen could arrive. A coordinated attack carried them all through, but resistance continued and grew in intensity as enemy rearguard units attempted to cover the German retreat. On the Fifth Army's right flank the FEC had relieved the 3d Division in the area near Palestrina. The 3d then shifted westward to form the right flank of II Corps just south of the Aniene River.

In an effort to shore up the Fourteenth Army and hold open the Aniene River crossings, Kesselring attached the 15th Panzer Grenadier Division to LXXVI Corps. His concern was for the Fourteenth Army units still south and west of Rome and in the Alban Hills. "Consequently," says the official history, "during the night of 3 June, with the 15th Panzer Grenadiers providing a shield, General von Mackensen managed to extricate the LXXVI Corps as well as much of the I Parachute Corps from the entrapment southeast of Rome."

While the Germans were concentrating on a retreat beyond Rome, General Clark and the Fifth Army had thoughts only of the Eternal City itself. As Allied forces approached the first indications of urbanization the excitement grew. It rose to fever pitch when the 88th Division reported sighting the Roman skyline. A Fifth Army staff officer at the headquarters commented that "the CP has gone to hell. No one is doing any work here this afternoon. All semblance of discipline has broken down."

Clark, in his concern for the Tiber River bridges, ordered the II and VI Corps commanders to form mobile task forces to advance into the city and seize the spans before the Germans could destroy them. They could not know that, only hours earlier, Adolf Hitler himself had given Kesselring orders not to demolish the bridges. Fifth Army spearheads thus pushed forward.

"The tactical progress of the Fifth Army's many spearheads during the last few hours before the army entered Rome," says the official history, "formed confusing patterns as the small, highly mobile armor-infantry task forces leading the two corps toward the city darted back and forth through the multitude of roads and alleys veining the Roman suburbs."

168

Men of the 85th Division march through a Roman gate (Porta Maggiore)

The main body of troops was to halt at the outskirts until the bridges were secured.

Task forces belonging to II Corps—one under Frederick, consisting of the 1st SSF and the Howze task force, the other from 85th Division resources—were up front in the advance on Rome. The 1st SSF units encountered fierce enemy fire near the suburb of Centocelle, three miles east of Rome. German 150-mm guns held Howze's tanks there as well. By daybreak of 4 June a unit of the 88th Division (attached to Frederick's force) had penetrated the city's outskirts along the Via Prenestina, but pulled up to await reinforcements. Other units, bypassing the firefight at Centocelle, were stopped by German antitank artillery. While the bulk of the SSF was being held at Centocelle, its 1st Regiment swung cross-country to enter another eastern suburb of Rome, Tor Pignatara. Clinging to the decks of their tanks, the 1st Regiment's Company H led the way. General Frederick and his subordinates followed with Companies I and C. "Until this column reached the outskirts of Rome," reports the official history, "the main obstacle was a crowd of newspaper correspondents and an American field artillery battery in convoy."

Driving on through Tor Pignatara the 1st Regiment, within an hour, crossed the city limits of Rome. The lead tanks had hardly passed over the line when an antitank gun opened up, sending infantrymen and correspondents scurrying for cover. Two American tanks were destroyed before the Germans withdrew. Moving on, the Allies were warned by civilians of mines and an ambush. Just as Frederick was preparing to bypass this obstacle, Generals Clark and Keyes arrived. Companies I and H were sent to outflank the ambush and, catching the Germans off guard, destroyed nine armored vehicles before the enemy fled. Advancing northwest, they made contact with the 1st Regiment's Company G on a steep bank. Passing below was the German force which had held up the bulk of the SSF at Centocelle. The men of Company G quickly prepared an ambush, only to discover that they could not depress their guns far enough to hit the enemy column below. The Germans, on the other hand, could not elevate their guns high enough to fire on Company G, and passed on into the city. At that moment Colonel Howze arrived with his column and prepared to dispatch a tank-infantry force to seize the bridges in his zone of responsibility. At 1530 Howze's column began to move, led by numerous tank-infantry patrols, each with instructions in the Italian language calling upon Romans to lead them to the Tiber bridges.

Even on June 4 there is action on a Roman street

Back at Tor Pignatara another unit of the 1st Regiment arrived and was led by the Romans around German strongpoints. At one point a squad entered an apartment building and, riding the elevator to the top floor, used a bedroom window as an overlook to kill a sniper. The squad then paused a moment to enjoy the cool drinks and sausage offered them by the inhabitants of one of the apartments.

Howze's tank-infantry patrols had taken their bridges by midnight, and other detachments were making their way to the Tiber. A battalion of the 88th Division, traveling in the darkness, attempted to seize a bridge already held by the 1st SSF. Each mistook the other for the enemy, and during the short firefight that followed General Frederick was wounded for the ninth time—"thereby easily establishing himself as the most shot-at-and-hit general in American history," noted one observer.

Following the 1st SSF, Task Force Howze and the 88th Division attachments, the 3d and 85th Divisions advanced to take up positions in the city. The 85th Division, on orders from II Corps headquarters, sent the 337th Infantry south along Highway 7 to trap the German forces in front of VI Corps. Arriving at the highway at 1700, the infantry found the 1st Armored Division already there. An 88th Division task force siezed the Ponte Cavour, and to the north the 3d Division took the railway bridge which crossed the Aniene River in the northeast quarter of the city. By 2300 that night (4 June) II Corps had secured all the bridges in its zone.

VI Corps, in the meantime, kept a slower pace. At dawn on 4 June the 1st Armored Division's Combat Command A was moving slowly through the outskirts of Albano, when word arrived at corps headquarters of II Corps's rapid advance. Realizing the enemy had withdrawn, Harmon was given the green light to pursue. By 1800 that day CCA was through the Porta San Giovanni and into Rome. CCB encountered active rearguard strongpoints but finally fought its way to the city's outskirts. By nightfall the 1st Armored Division had seized the bridges in its sector and reached the western edge of the city. The 36th Division, which had led the breakthrough at the Caesar Line, reached the Italian capital that evening along the Via Tuscolana. While the division progressed to the bridges already secured by Harmon's armor, General Walker said later, "along the dark streets we could hear the people at all the windows of the high buildings clapping their hands."

General Clark then arrived and, leading the official party, gathered his victorious commanders together at the Capitoline Hill, on Benito Mussolini's balcony. His speech began, "This is a great day for the Fifth Army . . ."

In Context

World War II was almost four and a half years old when the Allies landed at Anzio. Although some historians (and with good reason) date the beginning of the war from the outbreak of fighting between the Japanese and Chinese in 1937—and this fighting itself was actually part of a story that had been evolving since 1931—the usual date for the coming of the war is 1 September 1939, when at dawn the armies of Adolf Hitler opened hostilities against Poland.

It was a quick, victorious campaign for the Germans. Then, in 1940—protected in the east by a treaty with Russia (the Nazi-Soviet Pact)—Hitler swept through western Europe in an amazing march of conquest: Denmark, Norway, the Netherlands, Luxembourg, Belgium and, to the world's shock, France. The Führer seemed all-conquering. But his remaining foe, Britain, was an island protected by a navy and an air force. The German armies could not cross water, unless they were ferried over it in boats and protected by air superiority. The Battle of Britain, fought in the summer of 1940, was waged to determine control of the air over England. The German Luftwaffe lost—and the war went on.

In 1941, Hitler—for reasons that have been much discussed—turned east again, sending his armies into the Soviet Union on 22 June. Britain and the still-neutral United States sprang to Russia's aid with lend-lease munitions and supplies. Then, in December, with the Germans stopped at the gates of Moscow, one of the most dramatic events of the century occurred: Japanese aircraft, flying from carriers, attacked the U.S. naval and military bases in Hawaii, and with the slogan "Remember Pearl Harbor!" the United States entered the war. Germany and Italy followed with declarations of war on the United States, although they had not known of the Japanese plan, and the war became truly global.

Even though it was a Japanese attack that had propelled the Americans into the war, they adhered to previously drawn-up plans which called for the main effort against Germany, the life and soul of the Axis coalition. Then, after the Germans were beaten, the Allies could turn all their might against Japan.

Thus it was that in the fall of 1942 the Anglo-Americans landed in northwest Africa, where his book picks up the story—from Africa to Sicily to the first landings in Italy. And then to Anzio. For the British the Italian landings were perhaps especially significant, for they represented a return to Europe by the army that, in 1940, had almost miraculously been evacuated from the Continent after the Germans had broken the Allied front in France.

And so, when on 9 June 1944 Winston Churchill sent his congratulations to all those instrumental in leading the Allies to Rome, it must have been an exultant moment for the British leader. But in these same days other great events were taking place. On 6 June, Overlord, the Allied invasion of German-held Normandy, had begun, and the eyes of the world were turned to northern France—then to southern France, where further Allied landings were made—and then to the Allied armies as they moved toward and, ultimately, into Germany.

The Italian theater came to seem almost a forgotten part of the drama; reinforcements went to the armies in France. But the Allied generals and infantrymen continued their offense as best they could until finally, in the spring of 1945, both the Fifth and the Eighth Armies reached the Po Valley. Germany was now finished. On 2 May 1945, just a few days before their general capitulation to the Allies, the Germans in Italy surrendered to the opponents who had struggled against them since 1943 in some of the grimmest fighting of the war.

By this time Allied forces had reached across the Pacific to the doorstep of Japan. (Some high points of the Pacific war are described in three Men and Battle books—*Tigers Over Asia; Carrier Victory: The Air War in the Pacific;* and *Okinawa: The Great Island Battle.*) Allied leaders contemplated a bloody invasion of the Home Islands, even though Japan's shipping was gone and a great American air offensive was devastating her cities.

But there was no invasion. There were, instead, atomic bombs on two middle-sized cities, Hiroshima and Nagasaki. And on August 14 the Japanese surrendered. World War II, the truly global war, was over.

For Further Reading

ADLEMAN, ROBERT H., and WALTON, GEORGE. *Rome Fell Today.* Boston: Little, Brown, 1968.

BROWN, ANTHONY CAVE. *Bodyguard of Lies.* New York: Harper & Row, 1975.

BLUMENSON, MARTIN. *Anzio, the Gamble That Failed.* New York: J. B. Lippincott, 1963.

——. *Salerno to Cassino* (U.S. Army in World War II series). Washington, Office of the Chief of Military History, 1969.

CHURCHILL, WINSTON S. *The Hinge of Fate* (The Second World War series). Boston: Houghton Mifflin, 1950.

——. *Closing the Ring* (The Second World War series). Boston: Houghton Mifflin, 1951.

CLARK, MARK W. *Calculated Risk.* New York: Harper, 1950.

CRAVEN, WESLEY FRANK, and CATE, JAMES LEA. *The United States Army Air Forces in World War II* (Vol. 3). Chicago: University of Chicago Press, 1951.

EISENHOWER, DWIGHT D. *Crusade in Europe.* Garden City, N.Y.: Doubleday, 1949.

FISHER, ERNEST F., JR. *Cassino to the Alps* (U.S. Army in World War II series). Washington: Center of Military History, 1977.

GARLAND, ALBERT N., and SMYTH, HOWARD MCGAW. *Sicily and the Surrender of Italy* (U.S. Army in World War II series). Washington: Office of the Chief of Military History, 1965.

GREENFIELD, KENT ROBERTS (ed.). *Command Decisions* (U.S. Army in World War II series). Washington: Office of the Chief of Military History, 1960.

HISTORICAL DIVISION, DEPARTMENT OF THE ARMY. *Anzio Beachhead* (Armed Services in Action series). Washington: U.S. Government Printing Office, n.d.

LINKLATER, ERIC. *The Campaign in Italy.* London: His Majesty's Stationery Office, 1951.

MAJDALANY, FRED. *Cassino, Portrait of a Battle.* Boston: Houghton Mifflin, 1952.

MATLOFF, MAURICE (general ed.). *American Military History.* Washington: Office of the Chief of Military History, 1969.

MAULDIN, BILL. *Up Front.* New York: Henry Holt, 1945.

POGUE, FORREST C. *George C. Marshall, Organizer of Victory 1943–45.* New York: Viking, 1973.

PYLE, ERNIE. *Brave Men.* New York: Henry Holt, 1944.

SHEEHAN, FRED. *Anzio, Epic of Bravery.* Norman: University of Oklahoma Press, 1964.

TRUSCOTT, LUCIAN K., JR. *Command Missions.* New York: Dutton, 1954.

WINTERBOTHAM, F. W. *The Ultra Secret.* New York: Harper and Row, 1974.

Index